Productivity for Librarians

CHANDOS
INFORMATION PROFESSIONAL SERIES

Series Editor: Ruth Rikowski
(email: Rikowskigr@aol.com)

Chandos' new series of books are aimed at the busy information professional. They have been specially commissioned to provide the reader with an authoritative view of current thinking. They are designed to provide easy-to-read and (most importantly) practical coverage of topics that are of interest to librarians and other information professionals. If you would like a full listing of current and forthcoming titles, please visit our website www.chandospublishing.com or email info@chandospublishing.com or telephone +44 (0) 1223 891358.

New authors: we are always pleased to receive ideas for new titles; if you would like to write a book for Chandos, please contact Dr Glyn Jones on email gjones@chandospublishing.com or telephone number +44 (0) 1993 848726.

Bulk orders: some organisations buy a number of copies of our books. If you are interested in doing this, we would be pleased to discuss a discount. Please email info@chandospublishing.com or telephone +44(0) 1223 891358.

Productivity for Librarians

How to get more done in less time

SAMANTHA HINES

Chandos Publishing

Oxford • Cambridge • New Delhi

Chandos Publishing
TBAC Business Centre
Avenue 4
Station Lane
Witney
Oxford OX28 4BN
UK
Tel: +44 (0) 1993 848726
Email: info@chandospublishing.com
www.chandospublishing.com

Chandos Publishing is an imprint of Woodhead Publishing Limited

Woodhead Publishing Limited
Abington Hall
Granta Park
Great Abington
Cambridge CB21 6AH
UK
www.woodheadpublishing.com

First published in 2010

ISBN:
978 1 84334 567 1

British Library Cataloguing-in-Publication Data.
A catalogue record for this book is available from the British Library.

Typeset by Domex e-Data Pvt. Ltd.
Printed in the UK and USA.

Contents

List of tables

About the author

Samantha Schmehl Hines received her MS in Library and Information Science from University of Illinois Urbana-Champaign in 2003. She has worked as a cataloguer for the National Czech & Slovak Museum & Library in Cedar Rapids and as a reference librarian at Kirkwood Community College in Iowa City. Prior to receiving her degree, she worked for ten years in various paraprofessional positions. In 2004, she was hired by Mansfield Library at the University of Montana-Missoula where she is currently the Distance Education Coordinator/Social Science Librarian/Reference Desk Manager. Samantha is active in the Montana Library Association, Pacific Northwest Library Association, and the American Library Association. Outside of work she enjoys reading anything and everything, the outdoors, and time with her family.

The author may be contacted at:

Mansfield Library, University of Montana
Attn: Samantha Hines
32 Campus Dr
Missoula
MT 59812
USA
Tel: +1 406 243 4558
E-mail: *samantha.hines@mso.umt.edu*
URL: *http://libraryproductivity.ning.com/*

Acknowledgments

Thanks first and foremost to my husband, Eric, for his support and for reading endless rewrites. Now you know how it feels from the other side! Thanks also to Lorelei for taking such reliable naps. It was good to have a built-in two hours each day that I knew I could use. Mom and Dad, thank you for raising me to be a hard worker from the start. It really makes a difference in every aspect of life. And an extra special thanks to the Interlibrary Loan Department at the University of Montana Mansfield Library. I requested dozens of items while writing this book and you delivered over and over again.

Preface

In some ways I feel like a fraud writing this book. During the writing of this book I have suffered from the worst bouts of procrastination and writer's block I have ever had. The task seemed so huge and I felt incapable. I do not consider myself to be any smarter, better or more dedicated than the average person. In fact, in some ways I think I am quite lazy. I love to sleep, refuse to eat on the run or while I am doing anything else, and hate to take work home.

Then again, during the writing of this book, for which I had about a year to complete, I have made the following major accomplishments:

- celebrated my daughter's second birthday;
- got promoted at work;
- chaired a regional library conference (and made a profit at it!);
- took office as president of a regional library association;
- published a peer-reviewed journal article;
- went up for tenure;
- took on a supervisory position at my library;
- begun a reorganisation at my library;
- presented two sessions at library conferences;
- finished this book.

Most likely there were more things that I have forgotten. As much as I may feel I am not particularly accomplished, I can get things done fairly well without too much stress. I am good at getting things done, and perhaps that laziness is why. I value my spare time enough to not let work, or guilt about work, impinge upon it.

Much has been written in the past hundred years about personal productivity, from many perspectives. For a long time I have been interested in how to do more in less time and have read much on the subject. I have shared my thoughts and discoveries with others via conference presentations and essays. This book is an attempt to share that information more widely and broadly with a specialised audience – those working in libraries, with our particular time management concerns and issues.

I developed the ability to get things done at an early age. I credit my parents for the most part. They were great role models in putting work before play and then enjoying free time as much as possible. And, of course, I had chores to do from early childhood before I could enjoy my free time. I still remember having to weed the garden or finish maths assignments during summer vacation before I could go play with my friends or watch television. Although at the time I hated it, these life lessons have served me well into adulthood and the working world.

I began working in libraries when I was 16, shelving books at the library where my mother worked. The librarians there discouraged me from going into librarianship, saying that it would bore me. However, when I graduated from college with my bachelors' degree in political science, I ended up working for a public interest group doing their library relations. I soon learned that I hated working with politicians and politics. I then moved on to a law library support position, as it was located in the town where I wanted to live and paid a living wage. After a few months in that job, I decided to stop fighting the inevitable and go to library school. I received my master's degree in library and information science from the University of Illinois Urbana-Champaign in 2003. I found my current position at the University of Montana in 2004 and have been working here ever since. And I am hardly ever bored with librarianship! The field is always changing and growing, and I have loved working with people and information in a variety of roles.

As I approach tenure, I have written five refereed articles, one of which was co-authored, and I rarely attend a conference at which I am not leading a session or presenting a paper. I serve on several campus committees and in leadership roles in the library associations to which I belong. I do not say these things to brag; these are the things I need to do to progress in my position and meet my professional goals, and that is what I mean by productivity. I am certain there are plenty of librarians out there who have achieved more in less time, and do these things better than I do, but the important thing for me is that I am achieving my goals and enjoying my life. To me, that is the essence of productivity, not just producing articles, catalogue records, or subject guides as fast as I can. There is a bit of quantity to it, of course, but it is more of an issue of quality. I define productivity and success in terms of a balance. My ultimate productivity goal is to have a good work life and time for a good personal life. That is what I hope this book will impart to readers and, based on my research, this balanced approach is a fairly recent one.

What is productivity?

History of productivity

Productivity was first examined as a concept at the dawn of the twentieth century. In an attempt to boost profits and streamline manufacturing, labour economists started looking at why and how workers perform their jobs effectively. As they gained prominence as fields of study, management psychology and business studies soon began looking at these issues as well. During the 1950s and 1960s, when the USA experienced a boom in productivity as measured by worker output based on dollars invested in the business, a cottage industry sprouted up, promoting personal productivity to executives and business leaders. It was tied to the burgeoning self-improvement movement that bloomed in the 1960s and 1970s, which some say was started by Dale Carnegie's seminal work *How to Win Friends and Influence People*, first published in 1937.

For the first edition of Carnegie's book, only 5,000 copies were printed, but it grew dramatically from then to become an international bestseller. From a course on etiquette taught by the author to businesspeople, it grew to a worldwide phenomenon. The book contains one of the key lessons of self-help and productivity – change begins with the individual who wants change. Ideas on how to improve communication with anyone you may meet in the business world help establish the groundwork for getting things done effectively and efficiently.

This movement strengthened with the rise of the Asian economies in the 1970s and 1980s, especially as Americans looked to compete in the business world. With the advent of the internet and the information age, personal productivity has become a mania. Workers in every field, especially librarianship and information management, deal with issues of information overload and the acceleration of information-sharing. Dozens of books and hundreds of blogs now offer to teach you how to become more efficient and effective in your work life. This particular book will take a closer look at some of the more popular and enduring works in Chapter 5.

In preparing for and writing this book, I have read many of these books and blogs, and find that the perspective is beginning to shift a bit in the new century. While books in the 1980s focused on how to get the most out of your workday to free up time for your personal life and save money for your organisation, productivity resources are now beginning to consider a more holistic approach to free up time in all aspects of your life. Rather than focusing on productivity as a means to a more financially and time-effective end in your work life, in the past decade it has become more of a healthy lifestyle choice all around. It has shifted back from a profit motive to a self-help endeavour. More recent works have attempted to keep a focus on the business world and the practical implementation strategies of time management to avoid what can be a stigmatising 'self-help' label.

Defining productivity exercise

Now that we have discussed how others describe productivity, how do you, yourself, define productivity?

Take a moment to think about what you would hope to get out of a goal of 'productivity' and write it down.

Keep this definition in mind as you proceed through this book. You may differ a bit in your mindset but we should be talking about the same basic things.

This book will function best if, as a reader, you actually work through the exercises and questions, and commit your answers to paper or an electronic file if you are the sort who prefers computers to paper. The reasons for this are threefold. First, the act of physically creating a response to these prompts will cause you to engage with the material and ideas presented in a way that passive reading cannot. You will need to read closely and think about things in order to respond to the questions and exercises. Second, writing out your thoughts will allow you to gain perspective on your own thinking about the material presented and your life situation in a way that keeping it all in your head would not do. Finally, writing things down helps build accountability. Compared with keeping the information in your head, once you have a written goal or plan, it is harder not to follow through.

One of the main recurring themes in productivity literature is to get information out of your head and into another storage receptacle. Why not start with this book? Throughout the book there are prompts for recording responses to certain exercises – all you'll need is plain paper, a computer file or a notebook.

What productivity is not

Productivity is not just producing widgets as fast as possible. As information workers, most libraries have different metrics and assessments of productivity, so this is usually not too much of a mindset shift. However, there is still the impression that increasing productivity means producing more, faster. As alluded to above, improving productivity is about much more. Issues of balance and of quality are also part of the equation and this book will consider these in depth.

Productivity is also not about consuming information, although you may be confused as there is a plethora of information out there, with more coming out each day. This may sound odd, coming from a book devoted to making you more productive, but productivity is not about the book or the website you are reading or even reading more of these resources. It is about taking action. It is also about deciding what actions should not be taken, and working more intelligently to get the right things done.

In our workplace culture and in our lives in general, it seems that doing just one thing at a time is no longer enough. Workers are encouraged to multitask by working on two or more things at once. E-mails are read and responded to while we are in meetings, we take phone calls while reading the latest news on new products, or we eat lunch while working on reports. Even worse, we may take computers and cell phones home with us or on vacations and act as if we are 'on call' all the time.

Do you feel like you are able to provide your full attention to more than one task at a time? Most of us would honestly say no. Yet the pressure to multitask has become so high that it often feels an indulgence to close the office door, shut down the e-mail program, take the phone off the hook, and get some work done. We brag with co-workers about how busy we are and how much we have to work on. No one brags about how they produce better work faster when they focus on just one task or how they never have to take work home with them.

Later chapters will discuss multitasking and how to avoid it in more depth; the remainder of this chapter will however focus on library workers and why productivity matters to us. The next two chapters of this book will deal with issues of motivation, and then procrastination. After that, the book will explore time management – what leads to good time management and some tools for the tasks involved. Next we will talk about systems of productivity and what they can offer. We will then look at managing for productivity. Finally, we will examine ways to stay on track and stay productive.

Chapters will contain exercises to help clarify the points I make and relate them to your own situation. There will also be questions for consideration in each chapter, to further help with the application of productivity to your career. The book will close with a list of resources. Mention is also made of an online community (*http://libraryproductivity.ning.com*) to inform readers of new tools and tactics. Where possible, this community will also celebrate successes and work on overcoming obstacles.

Why librarians? Why libraries?

What makes libraries, and those who work in them, special? Why do they merit a whole book on productivity? There are three factors: de-professionalisation, the proliferation of information resources, and the growing expectation of immediate gratification by users.

Libraries are becoming de-professionalised in recent decades and much has been written on the topic. Budgets are tight all over, and one way in which libraries save money is by changing staffing structures. One worker often must accomplish what two may have done a few years ago, and sometimes this worker is at a lower level educationally or professionally than was the case previously. Reference librarians may spend less time on the reference desk as they take on more specialised tasks, like marketing, teaching, developing collections, and so on. The desk hours end up being filled by staff or students who answer basic questions and refer more specific needs to subject librarians. Cataloguers may be pushed into management positions while classified staff personnel perform the lion's share of actual cataloguing. In addition, the advent of the internet has led the general public to believe that they can directly find answers to their questions online without libraries at all and therefore reduce funding and other support, which further de-professionalises libraries.

While the amount and educational level of workers reduces, the information tools and resources library workers and people in general must deal with is increasing exponentially. We now live in the age of 'infobesity' (Bell, 2005), where library users can find overwhelming amounts of low-quality information with just a few keystrokes on Google. The questions that come to the desk are harder, as the easier ones can be answered, at least to the patron's satisfaction, with a quick internet search. And thanks to those quick internet searches, patrons now expect library professionals to answer their questions in the same speedy, overwhelming, and effortless manner.

Finally, those who use libraries, a number that in itself is increasing (American Library Association, 2009), are expecting immediate gratification. The internet and telephone have brought our libraries to the world, no journey outside the home required, and these services are based on an immediate response. Those who use libraries thus expect us to respond to their requests right away, adding further stress to an already stressful situation.

Libraries and productivity exercise

Think of libraries five or ten years ago. This can be from the perspective of your own position, if you have held it that long, or more generally. Make a list of the changes have you witnessed in staffing, tools and expectations.

This book is here to help. Presented in these pages are tools and information to help set priorities, manage your time, and empower you to do more with less. However, this book cannot change your life. If only it were that easy! You will have to want to change and commit to changing your behaviour. It takes effort to change your habits to be more efficient, but the rewards can be great.

Productivity cannot give you extra hours in the day in the literal sense. We all have the same amount of time per day. Many of us believe in the concept of making time, such as when a person says, 'I can't make time for this; I'm too busy already!' Unfortunately, there is no way for anyone to make time. There is only the time we have, and we all must learn to budget it effectively in order to take control of our lives. By following the adage of 'work smarter, not harder', we can perhaps free up time for better things. Controlling how you use your time is a powerful tool in reducing stress and getting more done, and it can be accomplished with a little hard work and dedication.

Why you?

To be reading this book you have some particular reason in mind. Some possible difficulties in your work life include:

- crisis management;
- disorganisation;

- inability to delegate;
- indecision or ill-considered decisions;
- interruptions;
- lacking clear goals or a vision for the future;
- meetings;
- no plan for your day;
- not knowing your priorities or how to set priorities;
- perfectionism;
- procrastination;
- trying to do too much.

There are three questions I would like you to consider as you work your way through this book. Again, this works best if you write down the answers on a separate piece of paper so you can refer back and reflect. Indeed, I would recommend a notebook or word-processing file for your exploration of productivity. Writing these things down, committing them to paper (or to computer file for those who no longer use paper), really does make a difference in how seriously you take these ideas and the thought and effort you put into addressing them.

- *Why am I reading this book? What do I want to change?* I make the assumption that in picking up this book there are some patterns in your life you want to change. Perhaps you are merely interested in doing more with the time you have, or perhaps you realise you have a real problem meeting deadlines and getting tasks done. Take a few minutes to think about this and have the answers in mind as you approach the rest of this book.

- *Am I committed to making a change in my behaviour?* The only way this book, or any programme, can help you be more productive is if you are committed to making a change in how you do things. It is perfectly acceptable to read this book out of curiosity or interest in the subject, but if you are expecting true change, you must be willing to put in some effort and time.

■ *What do I think will happen if I make these changes?* What are you expecting will happen if you become more productive? What is your vision of a more productive you? What do you think your work life and home life will look like? I ask these questions for two reasons. First, the answers can be incredibly motivating. To have a clear vision of the end result can help you put in the effort to change your behaviours. We will discuss this more in the next chapter. Second, you must be sure your vision of the future is practical and realistic. If you think this book can turn your life around, I would like to believe it will too – but depending on your circumstances it may require more than some changed habits.

Taking control of your time and focusing on being more productive overall can be a real blessing. In many of the books I have read, this is considered to be the best action you can take to control your career and your work life. In your work life, you may not have the chance to be your own boss in the professional sense, but you control your goals and what you accomplish at work in a very real and important way. When it comes to your career, this book can help you truly become the master of your fate.

This book should be used as a guide in whatever way works best for you. You can read the whole thing straight through. You can read the sections that interest you and are most relevant to your life. You can skim it for tips and tricks. You can visit the website offering continuing information on libraries and productivity. Any step toward productivity is a positive one.

2

Motivation

It is much easier to increase your productivity if you have a reason to do so – a motivation. Common drivers of productivity include family, career success, fame and fortune. It just feels better to focus on improving yourself, your career, your family time, and so on, rather than simply 'increasing productivity'. Such a generic notion fails to be motivating for most people. This chapter will help you identify your motivations, set up goals, and discuss work-life balance and burnout. You will also learn about setting limits and using some simple techniques to make it easier to get things done. But to begin, it is easier to get things done if you care about getting them done – if you can see the big picture.

The big picture and setting goals

Much has been written about the benefits of setting goals. This exercise is a similar endeavour. To feel motivated to be productive in your work, it is essential to know what you are trying to accomplish overall. Why are you working in a library? What is it that you hope to get out of your career? Why do you stay here? What is your passion?

This exercise works best if you are honest. If you are looking for a paycheque, write that down. Keep in mind that a reliable paycheque probably depends on you doing your job well, so it is a legitimate motivation. If working with the public inspires you, put that down. If you are looking to be promoted or achieve tenure, put that down.

Now that we have written down the big picture, what will it take for you to make or keep it a reality? These will be your actual goals. In order to be motivational, goals should be achievable and specific. If your goal is to be Director of the Chicago Public Library System in five years and you are just starting library school, you are likely setting yourself up for failure and frustration. A better and more achievable goal might be a full-time professional library position within one year of receiving your degree.

In addition, beware of too much specificity. It helps if your goals can be accomplished simply. For example, setting your sights on the Chicago Public Library System directorship may be a bit too specific if you have no prior connection to them, especially given the number of library school graduates in the area. Perhaps you could imagine yourself with a full-time job in the Midwest USA within one year.

Goals should be learning objectives and guide your actions in a positive way that leads to the development of skills or knowledge. Goals should not reduce these actions to a problem that must be solved. An example is if you have a goal to hit a certain salary. Once you have reached it, you will likely no longer be motivated to learn and grow as a library worker. You have reached your monetary limit and may enter a holding pattern until retirement. And from another angle, what if you never hit that salary level? This goal may distract you from some real learning experiences and failing to meet it may lead to a lack of appreciation for what you have achieved.

Once you have thought of some smaller and more tangible goals to help you achieve your big picture, write them down. Three goals is a good number to aim for, but more or fewer is just fine as well.

For me, an important goal is achieving tenure at my institution. However, it would be most useful for me to break this down into smaller goals or action items – publish a book, cultivate letters of support, serve in a position of leadership in a library association. From there we can break things down even further – develop an idea for a book, research the topic, create an outline, send it to publishers. The best goals are those that are actionable – where you actually *do* something to achieve your goals. Once goals these are achieved, they should be replaced with new goals to continue motivating you to learn more and do more.

SMART goals

Another way to approach goal-setting is via the acronym SMART. Tossed around the business world for decades, SMART goals should be:

- *Specific*: We covered this above. The objectives of your goal should address a specific action to be taken. You may want to use action words. Rather than 'be employed', I may choose to 'accept a position at a large research university in the Western USA'. Again, too much specificity may make your goal too difficult to attain.

- *Measurable*: To achieve your goals, you need to know how you will tell that you have succeeded. Say that my goal is 'to be a success in the library world'. How could I tell that I have done that? It may be better to set my goal as to 'write the seminal work on reference services in the twenty-first century'.

- *Achievable*: So I want to write that seminal work on reference services, but how much experience and knowledge do I have in the area? How much have I written? How well known and regarded am I? It might be better to have a more achievable goal of 'write a well-received article on an aspect of reference services in the twenty-first century'.

- *Relevant*: I work in a reference department in an academic library, so the goal of writing an article addressing reference services is definitely relevant to my day-to-day activities and interests. This may not be the case if I worked in a different type of library or a different position. Your institution's goals and aims are important to take into account as well.

- *Time-bound*: The best goals have a set end date or time-related milestone. This helps to reduce procrastination and ensure you actually accomplish your goal. I could have the goal of writing that reference article, and not get to work on it until I retired. Time is a definite motivational factor.

Take your goals from the big picture exercise, and rework them to meet the SMART guidelines. How do they differ?

What if I have no goals?

Some of us may not have very many goals in life in our particular circumstances. Can you still be productive and accomplished without goals? Sure. I recommend goals, especially higher-level life goals, because they do so much to inspire us, but I have been in situations in my life where my goal was simply to continue on until the next day. I have also been in less bleak situations, where my goal was simply to keep on doing what I was doing. Goals definitely do not need to be on the higher level or even exist to achieve productivity.

Do not discount the factor motivating your goals, whatever it may be. Like I said earlier, 'continuing to receive a paycheque' has kept me productive through many months of otherwise unrewarding work. Another thing to think about is that you can have goals that are less positively constructed. We have discussed a lot of higher-level goals like achieving tenure or a directorship. Perhaps you know that management is *not* for you, or you know that you have no desire to be a cataloguer. Thinking about what you do not want out of your work life can lead you to set some goals that can motivate you. And this is really what the goals are there to accomplish – to motivate you and drive you forward in your career. If you are content with where you are now, then you have no need to worry about your present lack of goals. You can always set them later if you feel this might be beneficial.

A final thing to do if you feel you are in a holding pattern or have no direction in your career is to talk to a supervisor or trusted mentor if you have one. People with experience in the field can help guide you in ways that no one else can. If you have no one in your institution with whom you feel you can talk, try joining a library association and finding a mentor there. Many associations have mentoring programmes to help newer librarians and library workers figure out their path in the profession.

Achieving balance

However actionable and well-thought out your career goals are, you cannot work on them all the time. A very important aspect of motivation and productivity, and one that is often neglected when discussing careers, is balance. You will be much more productive at your job and a happier, healthier person in general if you are not working all the time. Conversely, your personal life can also impinge upon your work performance. The information in this chapter can help you gain and maintain equilibrium between these two important spheres.

When dealing with goals and workplace pressures, you will not always feel incredibly motivated, and a feeling of balance can help you press on with work even through periods where motivation may be lacking. Having a balance between work and your outside life will help regulate and deal with these natural rhythms in motivation and protect against burnout, which we will discuss in a moment.

Work-life balance exercise

Productive people tend to view themselves holistically. It is common to suggest that work and personal life should remain separate spheres, but this is not always realistic. They need to be considered concurrently and a balance needs to be reached. While the previous exercise focused on the big picture of your work, this exercise will bring in outside forces such as your family, hobbies and other pursuits.

Make a list of the commitments in your life that are absolutely necessary for you. If you volunteer for two hours a week at a particular organisation and find this essential to your self-image, put that down. If you must have dinner as a family every night, put that down. If the best part of your job is working directly with patrons, put that down. Answer the questions: What am I committed to? What fulfils me? What is essential? This should not be a long list. Try to limit yourself to five items or fewer.

The flip side of the coin is to examine what you are doing already, either personally or professionally, and ask yourself what you are willing to give up. These can be hard choices, things you love, but ultimately things that are not essential.

Sometimes it can be very easy to think of these things, as they suck away the motivation we have for our jobs.

The point is that, as much as we might like to do so, we cannot do everything, all of the time. Most of us overestimate the amount of time we have available. Indeed, it is worth recalling Hofstadter's Law: 'It always takes longer than you expect, even if you factor in Hofstadter's Law' (Hofstadter, 1999: 152). In most situations, we can give up something to some extent to release more time for our true commitments.

For me, my primary commitment is my family. My job's primary purpose is to put a roof over their heads and food on the table, and to allow me to be home most nights and weekends. A secondary commitment is working directly with students and feeling like I am actually helping them in their college careers. These are the reasons I enjoy working in my particular position.

When looking at what I do in the workplace, I chose to cut back heavily on traditional collection development activities. We are often taught in library school that we have to read reviews and stay abreast of publishing in our particular fields if we are to be effective bibliographers. However, with the transition in my library to an approval plan with automatic ordering based on profiles developed by teaching and research faculty in their respective subject areas, I have chosen to rely on the system to catch the important and relevant material for my areas and ask the faculty themselves to inform me of important new releases and updates in their fields to consider for purchase. This has freed up time for parts of my job that are more important to me and to the library. This was not an easy decision and it is not particularly popular with some of my colleagues, who feel the traditional, more hands-on approach is best, but it is a decision that works well for me. In return for the time and effort I am able to devote to parts of my job that I feel are more important, I am able to accept that perhaps some things may slip through the cracks collection-wise.

The answers from this exercise can help you realise your goals for your career and identify things you can perhaps do without. Ideally, you will be able to align your current life situation with these goals with a few changes. If not, this might represent a wake-up call, explaining why you may be struggling with productivity in your current situation.

How to achieve balance at work

One tactic that can help you achieve balance is to define your role with your employer from the start of your position, if possible, and set your schedule and workload according to that role. It is easier to set and keep limits from the start than to impose them later on, and it can be easier to clarify your role in a new organisation than to have to go back to the beginning. However, if you are in a position that you cannot or do not want to leave, it is definitely not too late to take this step to realign your work life with your goals and your employer's goals. Further, this step may be easier to take after a few months on the job, when you are familiar with how things work in this environment.

I have recently attempted this with my own workload. Due to an oncoming reorganisation I was stuck with a few too many duties and not enough time to do them. I met with our human resources director and our dean to figure out the alternatives and got some good ideas. It was difficult to admit that I was facing challenges, but most bosses would rather have work done well, or at all, and appreciate the chance to be proactive about potential problems. If your boss is not receptive or if you feel like your work life cannot balance well with your outside life or is out of line with your goals, this is a clue that you should perhaps consider leaving the position.

The key to a good work-life balance, and to a positive work experience, is to gain and keep perspective. What does your job mean to you, your profession, your organisation, your community, and the world? Fortunately, librarianship is rarely a life-or-death pursuit. We have the freedom to try new things in our jobs without too much trauma to our users, our employers and ourselves. It is important for us all to keep perspective of our own lives and needs, as well as for our libraries and librarianship in general.

One way to cultivate a good perspective is to consider your work life from an 'abundance mindset'. If you think of your position as one that provides you with opportunities rather than challenges, and take a moment to enumerate these opportunities positively, you will have a more positive outlook overall. A positive attitude and a sense of opportunity is a great motivator. Nearly every position provides some opportunity. If nothing else, our work environments help us gain experience in many ways – in the practice of librarianship, in how to manage employees effectively, in what we want out of our careers.

This is a chance to reframe how you are thinking about your current work problems to transform them into opportunities. For example, I might consider it a problem that my wage is low compared with the wage offered at peer institutions. Rephrased positively, this offers an opportunity to raise a request for a salary increase based on my work experience and data from the region. Draw up a list of your own problems and rephrase these as opportunities.

A good way to keep this perspective and to gain deeper perspective into your individual activities is to break up big tasks into smaller goals, as we discussed previously. Parcelling out tasks over time allows you to build up to your final result, seeing how your efforts take shape over time rather than rushing through in one big push. In addition, spreading the smaller goals over time can help us gain and keep perspective as to what our actions bring to our career and our libraries. For example, I had about a year to write this book. This timeframe, while longer than the average for a book, allowed me to reflect more deeply on what I was trying to say and how I was saying it. I had built-in times for me to go back, re-read what I had drafted, and add information that I had learned or experiences in my life to give some more perspective to the manuscript. It also allowed me to keep my work-life balance intact as I could more easily fit this slower-paced timeline into my workflow. This will be discussed more in the next chapter.

Some people find it motivating to distil their most important goals or commitments into a visual image to post in their workspace. This can easily be done with a small sign or computer screensaver. In my office I have a corner devoted to pictures of my family and a sign saying, 'Is this the best use of your time?' This reminds me to work more effectively in order to have more time available at the end of the day for my family. Others in my library have the library's mission or their department's mission posted where they can easily see it, to remind them what they are there for.

Yet another technique is to build a support system of colleagues and friends to help encourage you during difficult times and also share ideas on ways to overcome adversity. Librarians are great at networking and it can be an easy thing to find colleagues from your state, region, country or elsewhere with whom to communicate. This is a great benefit of joining a professional association. In addition, the larger view such a relationship provides can help with perspective. Just talking to another person about problems can help them seem smaller and remind you of your priorities.

Keeping balance outside the workplace

While work stresses tend to outweigh the personal stresses in many people's lives, in order to achieve and maintain an equitable work-life situation it can be beneficial to look at your personal life as well. Organisation and productivity habits should not stay at the office when you go home – think about how to apply some of the tactics from this book to your personal life as well. Could chores be more efficiently lumped together or delegated? Does your family need a better calendar or a to-do list? Is communication an issue? Do you need to set clearer limits with your family and friends as well as your co-workers? Are you a perfectionist in areas of your personal life as well as at work?

The primary goal of a good personal life is to be happy and healthy. Be sure your life outside of work includes plenty of sleep, exercise and healthy eating, as well as recreational and nurturing activities that you enjoy. Make sure your vacation time or time off from work is truly time away from the pressures of the office. Seek support for personal issues as you might for problems at work. Building a good personal life will reduce your risk for burnout at work and make you happier all round. Your personal life should be at least as important as your work life and you should work equally hard to succeed at goals for both. Be just as protective of your personal obligations as you would be of work obligations.

Burnout and setting limits

The main reason balance is so important is to prevent burnout. The *Oxford English Dictionary* defines burnout as 'physical or emotional exhaustion, especially caused by stress at work; depression, disillusionment'. It was first defined by psychoanalyst Herbert J. Freudenberger in 1972 and is a decidedly modern phenomenon. Its rise and prominence could be seen as parallel to the information age.

Dr Freudenberger identified an outline of 12 phases leading up to burnout (*Scientific American Mind*, 2006). These include:

- a compulsion to prove oneself – working beyond the point where others would give up, in order to demonstrate one's worth or value;
- neglecting personal needs – particularly not eating or sleeping adequately;
- withdrawal – becoming uncommunicative with co-workers or family and friends;
- depersonalisation – seeing those you work for and with as less than human, as interactions rather than people;
- depression.

Burnout is not necessarily about being overworked. It is more often about losing motivation and feeling unappreciated. It is occasionally a symptom of some organisational malaise, which we will discuss a bit more in Chapter 6. Burnout is best described as a sort of disequilibrium, and has an obvious impact on your productivity, not to mention your health and wellbeing. The best solution for burnout is to try to regain a sense of balance and of what is important.

To maintain a consistent level of productivity you will need to have some sort of break. Lunch breaks, rest periods and vacation times, all have their useful and necessary place in our work, but too often we do not take these breaks and thus end up even more tired and stressed out. The best way to head off or deal with burnout is to take as much break as possible. To be able to take these breaks when we need them, we will have to set some limits.

In my talks with fellow library workers, setting limits and saying no seem to be the most challenging part of becoming more productive. People are worried that they will seem like less of a team player, that they are mean, or that they are not collegial. However, if you are stressed to the point of not getting your work done properly, or neglecting your health or your loved ones, you are already going to seem like less of a team player and not so nice to be around.

Previous exercises in this chapter regarding motivation can be a great help in setting limits. If you know what your goals are and what you are trying to get out of your work, it can be easier to know where to draw the line. For example, if you have a project that requires some extra work, does it fit in with your goals and life to stay late or take work home, or will you have to make it fit within the regular work schedule? A good knowledge of your big picture can help make this sort of decision easier. Having a written position description including expected hours and spelled-out goals can help too. It can be easier to stick with things once they are committed in writing.

Another way to make your limits easier to set is to make sure your limits are as specifically drawn out as goals would be. It is much easier to stick with a defined limit, such as working only between 8:00 am and 8:00 pm, than something more wishy-washy, such as 'after work is done it is family time'. Obviously, your limits may still be tested by your job. Something may come up that requires you to come in early or stay late, but at least you will have a concrete limit that you can keep in mind when reviewing requests for your time or efforts.

To set limits on a day-to-day basis it is important to know how you work. By this I mean knowing if you work best in the morning, or in a group, or after lunch, or outside your office. Do you need quiet or a little bit of background noise? Do you need someone to bounce ideas off? Do you need long uninterrupted stretches of time for getting a task done all at once, or blocks of an hour or less to switch from task to task? Do you need your morning coffee or trip to the gym in order to function? Understanding your preferred daily routine and abiding by it is a key way to stave off burnout and reduce stress overall.

Daily routine exercise

Think about your ideal work routine. What would you do to prepare for work? When would you come in? What kind of environment would you work in? What tasks would you do when? When would you go home?

Once you have thought a bit about these issues, think about what would have to change in order to have your ideal work routine. What limits would have to be set?

Improving communication

Once you have identified some things that may need to change to move toward your ideal work routine, you should take some steps toward making these changes. Many of them will require communication: asking your boss to adjust your work hours, telling your family that you are not to be disturbed when you are working at home, and so on. This sort of communication can be frightening; people worry about being too assertive or about being rejected. One of the best books on workplace communication is the previously mentioned *How to Win Friends and Influence People* by

Dale Carnegie (1998). Despite its somewhat silly title, it presents an outline of how to communicate with grace and tact, yet assertively and professionally.

The book is organised into four parts. Part One presents 'Fundamental techniques in handling people' and sets forth three principles:

- do not criticise, condemn or complain;
- give honest, sincere appreciation;
- arouse an eager want in the other person.

The last one means to foster in another person a sincere desire to do whatever it is you are seeking.

Part Two of the book is 'Six ways to make people like you' and contains six principles:

- become genuinely interested in other people;
- remember that a person's name is the sweetest and most important sound in any language;
- be a good listener – encourage others to talk about themselves;
- talk in terms of the other person's interest;
- make the other person feel important, and do it sincerely.

Once you have succeeded in getting others to like you, you can attempt the next part: 'How to win people to your way of thinking'. This includes 12 principles, including:

- begin in a friendly way;
- show respect for the other person's opinion – never say 'you're wrong';
- if you are wrong, admit it quickly and emphatically;
- let the other person do a great deal of the talking;

- try honestly to see things from the other person's point of view;

- throw down a challenge.

This is probably the most vital section to our goals of productivity, as it demonstrates tactics to get another person on your side without any conflict or hard feelings. I highly recommend finding a copy of this book and reading this section at the very least.

Part Four of the book is called 'Be a leader: how to change people without giving offence or arousing resentment' and should be required reading for all managers. The principles laid out here are ideal for communicating with those we supervise, which seems to be an area sorely neglected in any sort of management training or education.

Many of us have trouble asserting ourselves and may feel that we are being selfish or asking too much. However, if making changes will boost our productivity and enhance our performance, and this can be explained well to those who will be affected, our limits will likely be respected. Improving our ability to say no can help with setting limits.

How to say no

Before moving on to the techniques for learning to say no, you must first recognise the need to say no. For many of us, this is the hardest thing – we feel like we are letting others down if we say no. Again, knowing why you are saying no, and knowing your limits, is a great starting point. It can help you to feel less like you are letting others down and more like you are supporting your own needs and your position's big picture. If you can articulate why you are saying no to others, it can also be helpful for their understanding and acceptance.

At this point, a key thing to remember is to listen carefully to what is being asked of you. Make sure you understand completely what is required, and also be sure you understand your position well and your workplace's priorities. As much as you may want to, if something is truly part of your job and your employer needs you *and only you* to do it, you may not have the option to say no. So be sure to understand the situation fully.

When you do understand the situation well and know that you want to say no to the request, you will need to do so in an unapologetic and gracious way. Apologising will make you look weak and may encourage the requestor to try harder for a yes. Remaining gracious is important so as to avoid those bad feelings that we worry may arise from asserting ourselves. Saying no can definitely be done poorly, but it can also be done well, in a way that makes all sides feel good about the decision.

One technique for saying no is to say instead, 'I will get back to you'. If a request for your time and/or effort is made in person or over the phone or in some other immediate-response environment and you feel uncomfortable just saying no, tell the requestor that you will get back to them. Say you need to consult your schedule, your boss, your to-do list – anything you need to give yourself some time to say no in a less immediate and more comfortable environment. This can obviously backfire if the requestor thinks the no can be turned into a yes or is not clear that you have just said no. Just be sure that you do get back to the requestor as soon as you can and that you are clear in saying no.

Another technique is to try to delegate the task. If you feel you are not able to carry out the request for whatever reason, suggest an alternative person. Perhaps a colleague would be more appropriate, or you know an up-and-coming intern or student. If you do this thoughtfully it can be a benefit for all involved as someone with a better skill set, more time, or the like may well be of more use to the requestor. Make sure that you are making an appropriate suggestion, however, and not just suggesting a name to end the conversation. If you can give the third party involved any sort of warning about the request coming their way, this is usually most appreciated as well.

A third technique is to practise saying no. If you are the type of person who simply has a hard time saying no, you will need to work to get used to it. If there is someone in your life you feel sufficiently comfortable with, like a spouse or a close friend, try some role-playing where you practise saying no in different ways. It sounds absolutely ridiculous, but it can be a great help to have already worked through a scenario or two and have some experience for when a real situation pops up. This is especially good for those of us who may have trouble responding quickly to situations in conversations.

A fourth idea is to think about what it might take to turn the 'no' into a 'yes'. Perhaps you are approached with an opportunity you would like to take on – a new project, a promotion, supervisory duties, and so on – but you know you do not have the time or energy as the situation stands now. Would having an assistant help? Would reducing some other duties make it possible? Perhaps a more flexible schedule could make it work? Explore with the requestor and your supervisor how you could say yes.

Engaging in a dialogue with the requestor and/or your supervisor can be beneficial all around, as you can explore what will happen if the task goes undone. You can discuss the importance of the task and perhaps find an easier way to do it, a way to fold it into another workload, or maybe discover that it could be scrapped altogether. Workplace priorities should be clear and open for discussion.

When you say no, it is important to have reasons for doing so and to know those reasons. The reasons do not necessarily need to be shared with the requestor, but they should be clear to you. When it comes to saying no, there is a feeling that we will disappoint someone. Either we disappoint the person asking for our help, or we take on extra work that will cause something else to slip, or we find we cannot get everything done well, or we lose our non-work time when trying to make up. For me, the key thing is not to accept a task that I know I cannot do well.

It has been suggested that gender plays a part in the ability to say no, and the library profession is a gendered one. Certainly it could be said that women feel more pressure to be accepting in general and may feel a need to prove something in the workplace that perhaps men do not. Such differences in the ways that men and women communicate, and the directness of that communication, have been studied thoroughly. In addition, the public service nature of librarianship also tends to attract helpful personalities who may find it difficult to say no. However, saying no is an excellent life skill that will serve you well within your career and outside of it. As discussed above, it would be impossible to do good work if you accept every request that comes along. You will soon be short on time and risk burning out.

Making your workspace work

Having a pleasant physical space to work in can also aid motivation. Keeping things clean, organised and relaxing in your workspace can save time in a few ways. Knowing where to find needed tools (stapler, tape, pens) and information (file folders, e-mails) will keep you from interrupting your work time and workflow to search for things. In addition, a tidy work area can prevent procrastination. Several times in the writing of this book I decided that my office needed a bit of cleaning before I could get to work. Keeping things clean from the start can eliminate this excuse.

We will hear more about keeping a clean and organised workspace in later chapters, but for now I will introduce you to TRAF. This acronym (like many others) is very common in productivity literature. It represents a handy way to remember how to deal with any piece of paper, electronic file, book, or other object landing in your workspace. To deal with the object, you must choose one of the four options:

- *toss it out*: if you will never need it again, get rid of it;

- *refer it*: if someone else could use it, give it to them;

- *act on it*: do whatever task the object represents, then toss it;

- *file it*: if it is too early to do any of the three actions above, or you want to hang onto it because you think you may need it, file it right away – it only takes a few seconds to file something.

There are dozens of filing systems out there. The easiest one is to just file things alphabetically by topic. Similar things can be done with electronic files, but searching technology is becoming so good with e-mail and computer files that it may not be necessary to create any sort of filing structure. It is a good idea to clean out your office regularly, and work through your files and piles with the TRAF acronym.

Think about your workspace with regard to your daily routine from earlier in the chapter. Are there ways that your workspace could be renovated to help improve your daily routine? Could things be changed to better accommodate your workflow? Something as simple as moving your desk to a different angle can help. In my office, my desk was positioned so that I sat with my back to the door, which I dislike. People would knock or even come in without my noticing their presence. Even though I had one of the few coveted offices with windows, I could not enjoy the view from any of the places I regularly sat and worked. In a fit of procrastination I got rid of my large computer desk and moved a small table next to the window and suddenly I had a very motivating workspace – lots of natural light and a nice view, plus I no longer faced away from the door. Not all of us are lucky enough to have an office with a window or even a door, I know, and some of us must also share workspaces. However, you may yet be able to identify possible changes that could help with motivation and workflow.

Finding the fun

One of the best ways to boost motivation and alleviate burnout is to remember, or learn, what is fun about your job, and try to emphasise that aspect. For me, working with students is the highlight of my position and something that becomes less and less common as I move up in my library. Working on the reference desk allows me to work with students directly, answer challenging questions, and learn what they are working on and learning about. If someone is looking for a substitute for their desk shift, I snatch it up whenever I can.

Another way to find the fun is to try something different. If you are lucky enough to choose what you work on, try to find a new project to occupy some of your time and energy. If your workplace does not allow that flexibility, try taking an evening or online class in a subject that is strictly for fun, joining a sports team or taking up a hobby.

If you enjoy spending time with your co-workers, this can help make your workplace more fun as well. As mentioned above, the signs of burnout include withdrawal and depersonalisation. Good relationships with your co-workers can help prevent burnout as you will be less able to withdraw yourself, and less likely to see those you work with and for as less worthy than yourself when it comes to rewards, assignments and the like. You do not have to become best friends or necessarily spend time together outside the workplace, but it can be beneficial to chat with colleagues about family, current events, and non-work-related topics. A friendly face can make it easier to come to work.

A focus on the future

The goals we set earlier in this chapter and the exercises we worked on to help motivate us can also form the basis of a review process. It should motivate us to see our progress toward these goals. This is yet another reason to write down things like our goals. Some people keep a notebook or a paper file in which they place their written goals and copies of any actions that they take toward those goals. For example, with my progress toward tenure I have kept a list of publications I have written, courses I have taken, sessions I have taught, thank-you letters I have received, and so on. I review these documents at least once a year when I go through my annual review process, but it has been helpful to look them over more frequently when I need to be reminded what I am working toward and what I am trying to accomplish.

Even if you are not required to complete any sort of formal review for your position, this information can still be helpful for that motivation. On top of this, it can be even more helpful for negotiating a raise, preparing an application for a different position, or justifying your employment in hard economic times. Review processes will be discussed more in Chapter 7.

Rewards

Most of the things discussed so far in this chapter have actually been a type of reward. Intrinsic rewards are ones that motivate you internally – meeting a goal is an excellent example of an intrinsic goal. Checking items off a to-do list can be a great intrinsic goal and we will discuss to-do lists in the next chapter. In some ways, the 'reward of a job well done' is its own intrinsic reward.

However, there are also extrinsic rewards. These are external and, often, tangible remunerations such as a pay rise, recognition from a supervisor, or a promotion. But we cannot rely on others to recognise our hard work and accomplishments all the time. One way to harness the motivating factors of rewards is to set up rewards for yourself.

During the writing of this book, I set myself the goal of writing 1,000 words per day. Some days it was incredibly difficult to motivate myself to write even that small amount. So I would give myself an incentive. If I wrote my 1,000 words, I would get to look at my RSS feed reader, or I could have a piece of chocolate, or any number of small things. With other tasks, the reward would be larger. When I was successfully finished with a conference I was co-chairing I took a week's vacation. My co-chair outdid me and took three weeks! I have not yet figured out my reward for achieving tenure, or for the publication of this book for that matter, but it will need to be something suitably grand.

These rewards can help motivate you in very clear and effective ways. Even if you are unlucky enough to be in a workplace where your praises are not sung or your job is not particularly enjoyable, you can still find some method to motivate yourself to work toward your goals. This ties in with our next topic, procrastination, where we will actually get started working on these goals ... eventually.

Questions to consider

- What are your goals? How will they move you toward your big picture? How will you reward yourself upon achieving them?
- Do you feel you are at risk of burnout? Why or why not?
- How are you as a limit-setter? Do you need to work on saying no? How do you say no now?
- How can your workspace be adjusted to be more compatible with your workflow? How can you make your workspace a place where you enjoy spending time and where you can get things done?
- How can you find the fun in your current position?

3

Procrastination

Procrastination became a constant companion of mine while writing this book. Prior to this endeavour, I usually had no problem getting things done, but some days working on this book was like pulling teeth. I tried everything to get out of writing. I kept checking e-mail 'just once more' or making 'just one phone call' or finding a need to rearrange my office. Many people think that procrastination is caused by having too much to do, or from stress. Most of the time, however, it is rooted in fear. The thought of being responsible for an entire book was terrifying for me, in a way that most of my work-related tasks are not.

To fall into the category of 'procrastination', a behaviour needs to be counterproductive, needless and delaying (Schraw et al., 2007). Delays in work faced by simply having too much to do can be a symptom of overwork or burnout and should be dealt with accordingly, as discussed in the last chapter. Procrastination also differs from simple laziness. With procrastination, you have the desire to do a task, which is missing with laziness, yet you desire to delay the task even more. Procrastination is usually accompanied by guilt and anxiety in a way that laziness is not.

Defeating true procrastination, like many other aspects of productivity, involves changing habits, thoughts and behaviours to become a better worker. If you are prone to procrastination, it is not enough to get rid of things to do.

You will need to commit to identifying the problem, making a change, and working hard on doing so.

Procrastination and perfectionism

Part of the 'fear factor' of procrastination can be found in perfectionism. The worst procrastinators I know are perfectionists. And most of us cannot do our tasks perfectly. So for perfectionists, getting started on a task sometimes translates, either subconsciously or consciously, into setting themselves up for failure. No one, but especially not a perfectionist, likes to fail. It is much easier and more comfortable to clean your office or file some paperwork or browse the internet rather than get started on a task. There is a smaller chance of failure at these chores and the stakes are not as high.

To become an efficient and productive worker, you will need to manage any perfectionist tendencies you may have. Wanting to do things just right is a good trait, and being aware of this tendency and asking yourself if the reason you are not working on a task is out of fear can sometimes help solve the problem. Realise that not everything you do can be perfect and choose consciously how you will produce your best work.

Perfectionism exercise

Worried about your perfectionist tendencies? Take this short quiz to see if you have a need to be. Give yourself one point for every 'yes' answer.

1. I set myself higher goals than most people.
2. It is important to me to be completely competent at everything I do.

3. If I make mistakes, people will think less of me.

4. It takes me longer than others to get things done.

5. If I fail partly, it is as bad as failing completely.

6. I hate being less than the best at things.

7. If I am not good at a task I want to quit it.

8. Other people do not work as hard at getting things right as I do.

9. I am not able to let things go – I tinker with tasks and projects past their deadlines.

10. I am frequently disappointed in myself and other people.

If you score more than five points, you may be a perfectionist. This may be something to address more thoroughly as you look to become more productive. Perfectionist tendencies can hold you back in work and in life.

Some steps that you can take include becoming more aware of your intentions behind procrastinating – is it due to a fear of failure or not being perfect? Try to become more mindful of any absolutist tendencies you have in other areas. You cannot expect 100 per cent all the time in any venue. You must choose how and where you want to be at your best, and how much effort to expend. You can appeal to your social or workplace support systems for help in curbing perfectionism. Ask them if your behaviour or thoughts are abnormal or just stemming from wanting to do your best. Ask them if the amount of effort you desire to put into a task is appropriate. Try challenging yourself to do something new or something that you think you may not be good at in a low-stakes setting. This can help you get over a fear of failure by allowing you to fail and see what the consequences are. For me, I am a terrible singer and dramatic performer. I got over a bout of perfectionism by singing karaoke. I was terrible but the audience loved it (luckily it was a short song) and I learned that failing at something is not the worst thing in the world.

Procrastination as avoidance

Procrastination is also brought on by a desire to avoid difficult tasks or things we do not want to do. Personally, I absolutely hate dealing with angry people and will do just about anything to avoid returning a call from an angry library user. Again, recognising the reason for procrastination is the first step in dealing with it positively. And in the case of difficult work, it is important to realise that the task is not going to go away. The angry library user will continue to be angry, and perhaps become even angrier, the longer I wait to approach the task.

It is important to note that procrastinating on a task is rarely beneficial. Procrastination increases stress by shortening the amount of time you have to devote to a task. In addition, the longer you delay a task, the more insurmountable it will seem. Most people with a procrastination problem know that procrastination is not a good thing, but it can be helpful when dealing with the problem as a whole to recognise how your habit is contributing toward your stress and workload.

Procrastination as poor impulse control

A new school of thought proposes that procrastination is a result of impulsivity. In our fast-paced gadget-obsessed social-networking society, we have so many demands on our attention that we have a hard time differentiating between what is important and what is immediate. In this situation, the immediate wins out and we end up reading e-mail 40 times a day, checking Facebook repeatedly, and chatting with co-workers rather than working on the report that is due at the end of the week.

Piers Steel, a psychologist at the University of Calgary, puts it in the form of an equation (see Kotler, 2009):

$$Utility = E \times V/I \times D$$

where *Utility* is how likely you are to procrastinate on a given task, *E* is the expectancy of success at the task, *V* is the value of the task, *D* is the sensitivity to delay, and *I* is impulsiveness. 'Expressed in words', says Stephen Kotler in an article on the theory, 'how likely one is to delay depends on one's confidence multiplied by the importance/fun of a given task, divided by how badly you need the reward [for finishing] multiplied by how easily distracted you are' (Kotler, 2009: 76). Professor Steel maintains that the largest variable in the equation is impulsivity and that impulsive people will have the most trouble with procrastination.

If you feel this may be the root of your problem, one way to minimise a natural tendency towards impulsivity is to visualise the future, to help make the not-so-immediate deadline more of a reality. Think about how accomplishing or not accomplishing your task will affect your concrete visualisation of the future. Realise also that giving in to procrastination to satisfy immediate desires will hurt in the long run. If you find yourself procrastinating because it is simply easier to check e-mail or any other more attractive and immediate task, take a moment to acknowledge that feeling of discomfort. Do not give in to the feeling, but allow yourself to feel it before moving on to the tips below.

How to minimise procrastination

The best prescription for treating procrastination is simply to do something – something work-related, that is. For example, whenever I caught myself checking my e-mail for the umpteenth time instead of working on this book, I would close down the program and make myself write a certain number of words or for a particular length of time before I could do anything else. I did not edit what I wrote. I did not go to a particular place to write, such as my office or my home. I did not wait for inspiration to strike or for the ideal situation. I just wrote for as long as I could stand to do so, but with an end goal and thus a stopping point in mind. Often I would find that, once the barrier of getting started was breached, I was willing to write for far longer than I was going to make myself do so.

If you have a list of things to do and find yourself procrastinating on all of them, I suggest tackling the most difficult or unpleasant one first. This way, the sense of success you will feel upon completing the task can carry you through some other ones on your list. You will know that the 'hard' work is done for the day and can let this boost carry you through your other tasks. Once I had completed the word count I was shooting for on this book each day, I usually felt energised and ready to finish some more tasks.

If you cannot bring yourself to start out with the most difficult, try the opposite and do the task that is easiest or quickest to finish first. With one victory under your belt it can be easy to move on to another. A librarian I know starts off his to-do list every day with 'wake up'. That way, he says, he can always check off something and feel like things are going well. Of course, this could backfire by leading you to feel that everything on your list should be so easy and thus cause you to avoid taking real action.

If you find yourself procrastinating because your work is unexciting, try challenging yourself to do it a bit differently. If you have a presentation to give, try doing it without PowerPoint, or having just pictures for your slides with no text. Change the layout for your reports. If you always check e-mail first thing in the morning, try waiting a couple hours to shake up your schedule a bit.

Defeating procrastination involves developing willpower. You will need to be aware of your actions and reactions, analyse your reasoning, and tell yourself to stop and refocus. Just like with telling others no, this is something that gets easier with time and practice. One immediate way to refocus your thinking is to remind yourself of your values and what motivates you. Realise that whatever emotion you are feeling is just a feeling and does not have to control your actions. Another key step is recognising why you are procrastinating.

Identifying procrastination exercise

This exercise will help you determine why you procrastinate. Write down the most recent three tasks on which you have procrastinated. Next to each, write down why you procrastinated – fear, avoidance, boredom or another reason.

Again, the important thing is to build up a resistance to acting on your emotions and develop willpower. This self-control will simplify many aspects of productive work as well as improve your life in other ways. Think of it as increasing your patience, which can serve you well in almost every situation.

Dealing with e-mail

When working on a project, most of us have to deal with a fair number of distractions, and if we are prone to procrastination, such distractions can prove irresistible. A key distraction is e-mail. E-mail is a great boon to modern work life, allowing us to quickly share information, ask questions and communicate intentions in a way that we could not have envisioned just a few decades ago. However, it has also allowed us to be interrupted nearly every second of the day, often with non-essential or confusing information badly communicated or sent to the wrong person. According to John Freeman in *The Tyranny of E-mail*, 'In 2009, it has been estimated, the average corporate worker will spend more than 40 per cent of his or her day sending and receiving some two hundred messages' (Freeman, 2009).

It has been demonstrated many times that e-mail has addictive properties. Checking your e-mail and being rewarded with a new message to read sets off a little thrill sensation in your brain – a sensation that is reinforced every time you get one of those many messages each day. Furthermore, the act of receiving an e-mail often leads to the creation of an e-mail, thus perpetuating the cycle.

Some choose to deal with the e-mail overload problem by declaring 'e-mail bankruptcy'. This is when an overwhelmed worker decides to delete everything in their inbox in the hope that if a message was truly important it will be resent. The worker promises him or herself that it will never happen again and that messages will be dealt with promptly from now on, only to find this method of dealing with the problem recurring time and time again.

Others have chosen to adopt various rules for reading and responding to e-mail. If an e-mail is not sent to the individual directly, from a mailing list for example, it goes into a particular folder or straight to the trash. Some choose to limit their responses to e-mail to no more than five sentences, in an attempt to keep e-mail as a short information-sharing tool and press other communications into forums such as telephone calls or face-to-face meetings. Some very brave souls have cut themselves off from e-mail altogether, setting up an autoresponder to tell those writing to contact them instead via phone or IM or Twitter. Unfortunately, this final response is not overly compatible with the library world.

In my opinion, the best way to deal with e-mail as a distraction is to shut down the program. Go ahead and close it. If you are unavailable via e-mail for an hour everything will be fine, and you will be far less distracted by the dinging and flashing that accompanies the software. If you simply cannot bring yourself to close the program, another tactic is to turn off all the alert noises and animations. This will keep you from reflexively looking at your e-mail every time the alert goes off, and allow you to be more mindful about when and how often you look at it.

I recommend handling e-mail like any other to-do task. E-mail is best managed when you set aside a specific time of day, or two or three, to check messages and either trash, refer, act or file. Hearing the constant 'ding' of your e-mail alert will drag you out of whatever you are working on. Along with many other productivity writers, I recommend that you preserve at least the first hour of your day as an e-mail-free zone to allow you to work on your most important projects when you are at your most fresh.

To dig yourself out of an avalanche of e-mail and get your inbox down to zero, so that you can begin to keep it clear and check it only at regular intervals, approach it like you would any major project. Set aside several hours. Prioritise your backlog and work through the messages following the TRAF acronym – trash, refer, act or file. Once you have dug yourself out, think of some way to capture the agony of the process and the good feelings you have now that your inbox is empty. Use that memory to keep you on track and working well with e-mail for the future.

Dealing with other distractions

Yet another tactic for dealing with distractions is to disconnect from the internet entirely while working. This takes care of all e-mail, instant messenger and web-based distractions. If you know you are prone to procrastination due to such interruptions, you may want to eliminate them as much as possible from the outset. There you can also install internet-blocking software on your computer. My favourite is LeechBlock, which allows you great flexibility in blocking out specific websites or classes of website for specific time periods. So, if you want to have your lunch-hour free to watch videos on YouTube you are allowed, but once lunch is over, LeechBlock or the software of your choice will prevent you from looking at the site. Other software limits the time you spend on particular sites to an hour or 30 minutes so that you can have time for research or a little break. The limit, however, keeps you focused on the task at hand.

Another common distracter is the telephone. It is tougher to silence but it still can be done. If you have the willpower, simply do not answer it. Otherwise relocate yourself away from the ringing or unplug the phone. Turn off your cell phone if you have one. Again, everything will continue to function if you are unreachable for an hour. And if it does not, consider discussing with your supervisor the need to reduce your workload or hire an assistant.

Distraction tracking exercise

For a day, keep track of what distracts you from your work, when and for how long. Be honest and thorough. If you are working on a task and the phone rings, a colleague stops by, or you just get sidetracked, keep track of what caused the interruption and how long it took you to get back to work.

The Pomodoro Technique

Another technique for avoiding distractions and beating procrastination is to set a timer for an amount of time and work on a task without stopping for that time. Do not do anything else – no checking e-mail, no web surfing to check facts (a particular failing of mine), and no answering your phone or your door. Allow yourself a short break when your time is up, then go back to work for a set time period again, perhaps on a different task. Try not to cheat! When your time is up, stop on the task right where you are. It can help you start again later if you were in the middle of a thought when you left off. You will have a natural starting point. In knitting they call this the 'rough edge' – the bit of yarn that leads you back into the project.

This technique has been formalised into something called the Pomodoro Technique, named after the tomato-shaped timer the creator used. Pick a task, usually from a written list, set the timer for 25 minutes, and work away. When the timer goes off, put a check on the list by the task and take a five-minute break. Then begin another Pomodoro, or 25-minute cycle. After every four Pomodoros, take a longer break. There is a website dedicated to the technique (*http://www.pomodorotechnique.com*) from which you can download a 45-page booklet that explains how the technique works and how to deal with things like interruptions and 'ring anxiety' relating to the timer at the end of a Pomodoro. You can even buy a tomato-shaped timer and tee-shirt for €30.

Procrastination as motivation?

In some situations, procrastination does not always have to be a bad thing. If you are avoiding a task and are aware of it, it could lead you to what is known as structured procrastination, or mindful procrastination. This is when your procrastination motivates you to do other tasks in avoidance of a primary task. This book was an excellent motivating factor for me with regard to my employees' annual reviews, my own annual review paperwork, the planning of two conferences, and several other tasks that seemed less onerous in comparison. The key is to keep a structure and know exactly what you are giving up when you complete certain tasks to avoid others.

Key to this structured approach and key to managing tasks in general (how else will you know what you are procrastinating from?) is the to-do list.

The to-do list

Some people cringe at the idea of a to-do list. They feel it is too structured, or that the tasks they perform do not lend themselves to a list. Others say that their job depends too much on having time to deal with situations as they come up and thus a to-do list is moot. Both of these are poor excuses. A to-do list provides needed structure to manage your time well. It allows you to take information out of your head and put it in another receptacle for safekeeping. The less you have to remember, the more mental energies you have available to deal with other aspects of your work. And if your work is such that your position is largely reacting to crises, you will need that energy more than ever. This is another situation worth addressing with your supervisor as it is not good for anyone in your workplace.

The to-do list offers a built-in reward structure. This plays upon motivation, as discussed in the last chapter. Checking off an item as done or reviewing a completed to-do list gives you an intrinsic boost, a reminder of your job well done. In addition, the fact that to-do lists help you keep track of what you have been working on and what you have accomplished can help immensely with seeking out extrinsic rewards like raises or promotions.

A key complaint about to-do lists is that people feel their job does not naturally lend itself to a list of tasks to do. This is likely not true. Your tasks may seem monumental or not easily quantified, however, even the most complex task can be broken down into manageable chunks that can be put on a to-do list.

An example is this book. I knew that, going into tenure, I wanted to have a book underway or completed. The first task was to come up with an idea. This was not a task with a firm deadline in mind when I started. It was a general goal that I had and I listed it thus when working on my motivations, like in the last chapter. Eventually, the idea to write a book about productivity for librarians struck me. With the idea in place, I could then break that into tasks.

First was the creation of an abstract or 'elevator pitch' about the book that I could use for discussing with colleagues or publishers. Second, I worked on an outline of the chapters, starting off with a general breakdown of the concepts I had identified in my elevator pitch and gradually increasing in complexity. I sent this outline to a publisher who was interested, and we worked a contract. At that point, the deadline pressure became a factor. Once I had a deadline, I broke the task into working on particular chapters, attempting to produce a certain word count each day for the chapter I was targeting. At least once a month, I went back and reread the work as a whole and made any of my friends or colleagues who were willing read it as well.

I would mark up a printout and dedicate a day or two a month to overall work on the book as a whole, then go back to my chapter-by-chapter approach.

Right now as I write this, I have a daily to-do list task of writing 1,000 words. If I achieve this goal three times a week I am happy and I know I will meet my deadline without too much last-minute scrambling. The key is that the chunks feel manageable in my schedule and are visibly contributing to the end result. Breaking down tasks into manageable pieces is a powerful tool for fighting procrastination. Faced with a huge, seemingly insurmountable task, it is much easier to procrastinate than with a list of short doable items.

A tip for writing the perfect to-do list item is to construct it along the lines of verb-noun-subject. So for me, this would look like: 'Write one thousand words for the book'. Other tasks I could put into this structure might be: 'Set up the reference desk schedule for the student workers', 'Create the outline for the Poli Sci 101 library session' or 'Gather vacation information for the desk schedule from the staff'. A few of these I could break down further. For instance, 'Talk with the Poli Sci instructor about online resources for the library session; print out handouts for the Poli Sci library session'.

An important point about constructing to-do list items is never to put an item on your list that you do not intend to do at some point in the near future. To-do lists should not serve as goals statements or reminders for tasks due in the far future. To-do lists should be limited to tasks that are timely, actionable, and something you will in fact be doing. If an action needs to be delegated, either delegate it straightaway or put the delegation of the action on your list.

You should also know why you are doing the things on your to-do list. If you have tasks for work that you perform but you do not know why, talk with your supervisor. Your boss should be able to offer clarification of the task's role with regard to the library and your position. If not, that might be a sign for both of you that the task is unnecessary or needs to be rethought.

Constructing to-do list items exercise

Take three of your current to-do items and write them in the 'verb-noun-subject' style.

Another tip is to create tasks that can be completely accomplished in one sitting. It is generally possible to write 1,000 words in a single sitting. On average, it takes me one to two hours. Calling an instructor to talk about a class can be done in one sitting, provided you can reach them on the phone and not leave a message. The above advice to time yourself and devote a set bit of time to a project, using the Pomodoro Technique, is a valuable way to look at your to-do list. Think of how you would define a 'sitting' (for me it is an hour or less), and break down your tasks until you get to that point. This will help later with time management.

Breaking down tasks exercise

Think of a large task or goal. Now break it down into tasks or steps that can be accomplished in one sitting. One of my favourite ways to envision this is as 'big rocks and stepping stones'.

To-do lists and organisation

One great strength of to-do lists is that, along with getting thoughts out of our heads and into another storage medium, they allow us to organise what we need to do and when we need to do it by. This can help us to be more productive by helping us group like tasks together, such as a list of phone calls to return. We can also arrange tasks by when they are due and see more easily which ones demand our attention soonest. We can have suitable tasks in reserve for times when we are waiting in line, riding the bus, or other 'wasted' times. We will revisit this in the time management chapter, but for now keep in mind how to-do lists and organisation can combat procrastination and increase efficacy.

To-do lists should not be exhaustive. As discussed previously, they are lists of actionable items that you personally intend to do. As such, they should be limited to no more than 20 items. As items are completed, new items will naturally be added, but if your list rises above 20 tasks, you will need to rethink how you are organising your list and if your tasks are perhaps better suited as calendar events (for actions taking place in the future) or as projects to be planned out and current, actionable tasks placed on the list as appropriate with deadlines and other information to be placed on your calendar or filed.

A key component to getting to-do lists to work is to set deadlines for your tasks. It may be helpful to list out all you need to do, but to make sense of it and make it work, you will need to know *what* is due *when*. Some of your tasks will have built-in deadlines, like annual reviews or assigned projects. With other tasks, however, you will need to become comfortable with setting your own deadlines and sticking to them. Treat any self-imposed deadline with the seriousness you would give to a deadline from a supervisor. If you know you have a problem with meeting deadlines, assign yourself a deadline earlier than the drop-dead date by when the task absolutely must be completed. With some training and hard work you can beat the urge to let deadlines pass by, and you will reap the rewards of less stress and more time.

If you procrastinate to the point where you miss a deadline, or several, you will need to talk with your supervisor or others who were depending on your work. If it is a habit with you, work with your supervisor to see if there is a solution to be found. Perhaps you need more people working on certain tasks or perhaps you are overloaded for your position. In any case, missing deadlines is a serious problem that will make your procrastination a problem for others, not just you. The next chapter, on time management, offers more advice to help you meet deadlines.

Deadlines exercise

Think of three pending tasks you have, perhaps from the last exercise. Assign them deadlines based on priority, how much time they will take, and your other duties.

Tools to help organise to-do lists

There are a number of tools to help you create, prioritise, share and store to-do lists, but right now there is one primary choice: paper or electronic?

Paper is standard and traditional for to-do lists. As long as you have a pocket or bag, you can carry paper anywhere, and you can add to it easily if you have a pen or pencil. Paper has built-in limits – usually whatever fits on the sheet – so it can help you instil limits on what you do. Paper does not require electricity or an internet connection. Paper is easy to modify however you would like and does not require any special training or have a learning curve.

There are a variety of paraphernalia out there that can make your to-do lists a little fancier than a regular piece of notebook or copier paper, although those work just fine as well. If you use Google to search for 'to-do list paper' you will get some excellent ideas, including my personal favourite, the Printable CEO series (*http://davidseah.com/ blog/the-printable-ceo-series/*). Mindtools also offers a nice template (*http://mindtools.com/pages/article/worksheets/ PrioritisedToDolist.pdf*) that is simple and elegant. Notebooks can be nice as they keep all of your tasks together and allow for a quick and easy review. Some people swear by the Moleskine brand, which comes in many sizes, paper types and colours, but others are just as happy with a spiral notebook, three-ring binder or legal pad.

There are downsides to paper as well. Paper can be forgotten or lost more easily than a computer or handheld device. Electronic to-do lists can be easily shared with colleagues or family. Electronic lists can often be easily reformatted, changed or rearranged. If you have a device like a smart cell phone or netbook that you carry with you and use, using an electronic resource can keep your to-do list more integrated into your workflow and therefore more effective. Electronic to-do list software can send you reminders within your workflow to make sure you do not forget important action items and deadlines.

If you decide to use an electronic to-do list, you will face even more choices. Would you like to use a web-based application? These are accessible anywhere, from any computer, but most require internet access. If you use a software solution, it may be tied to a particular machine or device, but this not a problem if you always carry such a device with you.

One of my favourites is the web-based Remember the Milk (*http://www.rememberthemilk.com*). It allows users to have multiple lists and share lists between users. You can send tasks to someone else's list as well. It keeps an archive of completed tasks and allows you to set due dates and create recurring tasks. You can make notes on tasks and postpone them as well. You can set up an RSS feed of your to-do lists, should you want one. There is a professional version with a few more features and also an app for the iPhone. As it is web-based, it can be accessed from any internet-enabled device, and it has an open application programming interface (API), which means that some developers have created applications for it that blend it with other tools, like Gmail.

Like several other webmail sites, Gmail itself has a built-in to-do list. Check for a link that says 'tasks' or something similar. These programs are usually fairly simple and easy to use. If you use webmail, this might be a good option as it would be in your regular workflow.

A couple other online to-do list/task managers as of this writing are HiTask (*http://hitask.com*) and DeskAway (*http://deskaway.com*). Both make their living by trying to sell you a more high-powered version or by providing free trials, but they can both be useful for figuring out what works for you, and they each offer great features like collaboration, logging-in from anywhere with internet access rather than a particular computer, and so on. A few more are listed in the resources section of this book.

As for software, if you are one of the many who use Microsoft Outlook for e-mail, this application has a built-in task management function. It is a bit complex to use, but there are resource guides on the internet and books available to guide you. I myself took a one-hour training session at my university on how to use it. The strength of using such a complex system is that you are already using the system for e-mail, so you may as well keep your to-do lists there as well. Second, the Outlook tool allows you to share tasks with others. This can be a big help if you delegate tasks frequently or work in a team structure.

I will caution you at this point not to use your e-mail inbox as a form of to-do list. It is handy and easy to keep incoming messages on which we need to act in your inbox to remind you that you have something to do. However, this separates tasks that come in via e-mail from all other tasks that you need to perform, forcing you to keep more than one to-do list. In addition, e-mail is a poor format for a to-do list. Messages are usually not constructed properly for actionable tasks or displayed well enough to serve as a proper to-do list.

Others have found success with maintaining lists in Excel. Excel has great flexibility in setting up rules for displaying and updating lists, creating and changing layouts, sorting lists, and so on. If you are familiar with Excel or need an excuse to learn the program, a to-do list kept there can be as simple or complex as you would like.

There are also a number of dedicated software programs for to-do lists based on systems, as will be discussed in Chapter 5, and for various operating systems, types of task, and so on. Running a web search for 'to-do list software' will bring up a list of them – some are free, some are not. I prefer solutions that are already within programs or systems that I use, but feel free to explore to see if others may work for you.

Getting started with to-do lists

The best way to get started with to-do lists is to collect all the tasks in your life that require resolution. I usually do this every few months just to make sure nothing is slipping through the cracks. I grab a piece of paper and write down absolutely everything I can think of that I need to do. Not only do I put down tasks that I am actually working on, but

I also put down future goals and projects I would like to start someday.

The next step is to figure out what on your list you do not actually need to do. If you need to set some limits or reduce some activities from your work life, this is a great time to do so. If you are working on tasks that are better suited for a colleague, now is the time to approach that person. If jobs should be delegated to one of your employees, do so. Put goals and future tasks on another list for a tickler file or other processing later. Only tasks that you personally intend to do soon should be on the list.

The third step is to organise and prioritise your list. Put like tasks together as discussed above, and/or make sure tasks related to a project or goal are grouped together. Then organise tasks based on priority. This can be based on impending deadlines, importance to your career goals or your institution's goals, and so on. Your view of the big picture that we discussed in Chapter 1 will come in very handy. We will discuss prioritisation more in the next chapter, on time management.

Now that you have your list, try out a tool for tracking your tasks. I would recommend paper to start as you get in the habit of keeping a to-do list. As you become used to the concept and as it works for you, think about trying a different tool that may mesh better with your workflow. We will discuss these a bit more in the productivity systems chapter and there is an excellent list of resources at the end of this book.

To-do list as tool, not lIfestyle

To-do lists are a tool to help increase productivity and help you maintain sanity by freeing up headspace for more important tasks. Keep your to-do list handy and visible. If your to-do list begins to overwhelm you or cause more stress than it removes, or its maintenance takes up more time than your actual work, then something is wrong with your system or your situation. A to-do list should serve as a way of organising what you need to do and when you need to do it. In this way it can counteract tendencies to procrastinate, by making it easy to see what you need to get done and make it feel doable. If this is not the case, please review the chapter on motivation and reflect on whether you may be facing burnout. It may also help to read on to the next chapter, on time management.

Questions to consider

- Where does your procrastination come from? Is perfectionism a problem for you? Are you avoiding difficult or unpleasant tasks?

- Have you used to-do lists in the past? Were you successful?

- Do you have a problem with deadlines, like Douglas Adams, who once said, 'I love deadlines. I love the whooshing sound they make as they fly by'?

- Do you feel like you will have a preference for paper or electronic tools? Why?

4

Time management

What is time management? I see it as ensuring that your time is under your control, that you are aware of how you are using your time, and that this use meets your needs. A large part of time management is time organisation and, beyond that, work and life organisation. In order to be productive, the key resource you will need is time, in big uninterrupted blocks. You can only achieve this by managing your time well.

Time management quiz

Work through this short quiz to determine where you fit on the spectrum of time management. Is this an area in which you may need extra help? Give yourself one point if the phrase vaguely describes you and two points if it really describes you. Give yourself no points if the statement does not describe you at all.

1. I take advantage of my learning styles and use the strategies that help me best.
2. I keep a calendar to help track my appointments and activities.
3. I keep all my important information (phone numbers, etc.) in one place.

4. I know what I prefer in my work environment (time of day, workspace organisation, noise level) and work under those conditions as much as I can.

5. I often review my goals and achievements.

6. I rarely double-book myself; I usually know what I have scheduled and when.

7. When I first get to work I take a few minutes to figure out what I will be doing that day.

8. If ever I feel overwhelmed by what I have to work on, I take a few minutes to organise myself.

9. I take good care of my health, eat right and get enough sleep.

10. I am able to put problems out of my mind and focus on work while I am there.

If you have 15 points or more, you are on the way to excellent time management. Nine to 14 points is about average. Anything below nine is cause for concern. You will want to think seriously about how you organise and track your time.

Plenty of people say they do not like the constraints of a schedule or calendar and that they prefer to be free to decide how to spend their time at any given moment. Perhaps for a few that works out well, but schedules allow you to control your time far better than going with the flow likely will. A well-constructed schedule will afford you more freedom to choose what to do with your time than the opposite ever can.

Key to this freedom is to realise that creating a schedule is something you do for yourself, solely for your benefit. Your schedule should serve you best. It can work with your natural workflows and rhythms to set up your work day in the best possible manner. Even if outside events are imposed upon you, like desk shifts, meetings and the like, the basic framework of your schedule will allow you to accept these requests upon your time gracefully and with less impact on your productivity. The first step toward realising your need for a schedule and figuring out how to make one work for you is to track how you spend your time now.

Time journal exercise

For one workweek, keep a diary of what you do when. At this point there is no need to attempt to set or follow a schedule. Just keep track from waking to bedtime what you do when. I suggest that you follow your entire day, not just your work day, to see if there are problems with getting out of the house on time in the morning, getting to bed at a proper time at night, and so on. This can also be done with time-tracking software, where you log how much time you spend on a particular task. A favourite of mine is toggl.com. For the initial exercise, however, I would recommend paper so you can easily cover an entire day without needing to access a computer.

Identifying peak productivity times

In the past two chapters we discussed how knowing your working rhythms can help increase motivation and prevent procrastination. An additional bonus of knowing how you work best is that it can guide you in the creation of a schedule. If you need the quiet and stillness of early mornings in the library to really get things done on writing projects, for example, be sure to schedule writing tasks for first thing in the morning. If you tend to be worn out at the end of the day and need a task that can hold your interest and that is rapidly changing, perhaps answering e-mail at the end of the day can do the trick.

To have a well-crafted schedule, you will need to revisit these workflows and see where tasks fit in best. You will then need to schedule tasks as you would schedule a meeting with co-workers. Think of it as a commitment to yourself to get work done. If your schedule has a spot devoted to writing your annual reports, it can be much harder to procrastinate or allow some other task to get in the way.

Once you know what you prefer to work on when, be sure to protect some of your key productive time for work on projects. Do not let others schedule meetings in this time and try to reduce interruptions and distractions. Work only on the task at hand until your schedule guides you to a new task or to a break. Schedule these as well. Skipping lunch and/or other breaks is an easy path to burnout, but much harder to do if you have blocked off sufficient time.

Here is an example of my schedule for today:

8:00 am: drop daughter off at day care

8:15 am: arrive at library

8:30 to 10:00 am: work on book, specifically editing Chapter 4

10:00 am to 12:00 pm: reference desk shift

12:00 to 12:30 pm: lunch

12:30 to 1:00 pm: assemble reference meeting agenda for next week and send out

1:00 to 2:00 pm: e-mail, prep for 2:00 pm meeting

2:00 to 3:00 pm: PAC committee meeting with head of systems

3:00 to 4:00 pm: texting reference shift, work further on book if nothing else comes up

4:00 to 4:45 pm: e-mail, set priorities for next day

4:45 pm: leave for day care

I am most productive in the early morning, before my colleagues arrive and before patrons start coming in and/or calling me. I try to reserve that first hour or so for the most challenging task I face for the day. That said, I do usually glance over my e-mail in the first 15 minutes after I arrive at work just in case I have to cover a shift or there is some other emergency that needs to be dealt with. I do not dive into e-mail, however, until the early afternoon. I usually find my energy a little low after lunch, so e-mail is a good post-lunch task for me. You will note that I did schedule in a lunch break. I cannot recommend this highly enough. Ensuring that you get at least one break is very important for productivity.

While I have a plan for every hour that I'm in the office, I try to budget extra time to deal with emergencies. You can see an example of this at 3 pm. Our text message reference program does not have high traffic levels so I can usually do something else during the same time – this is known as smart multitasking and will be discussed later in the chapter. If nothing else comes up, I can continue working on this book, but if something does arise that must be dealt with, I can squeeze it in easily.

How to get out the door at the end of the day

You may also note that I have a firm time to leave scheduled into my calendar. In many ways I am fortunate to have a commitment every evening after work. If I do not pick up my daughter by a certain time, I will have to pay a penalty that increases by the minute – an excellent motivation to get out of the office on time.

While I can honestly say this has never been a problem for me, many of my colleagues do have a problem leaving the library in a timely manner each evening, and scheduling a commitment after work can definitely help. Family dinners, yoga classes, and so on can help you leave work on time as well as oblige you to find time for an activity you enjoy.

Another tactic is to set an alarm to go off at the time you wish to leave. Such a reminder is effective if you are the sort of person who glances up at the clock and wonders where the time went and how you stayed so late again. If you don't have a traditional alarm clock, various computer programs will serve as an alarm, including most calendar software.

A tip that serves us well from many perspectives is to work on your most important tasks early in the day. This way, when quitting time rolls around, you know you have accomplished your goals for the day and feel good about leaving. If you do not start working on needed tasks until the afternoon, you may end up feeling the need to continue working past the time at which you would like to leave.

One of the best ways to ensure you leave work on time with your work done for the day is to defend your time against interruptions. A daily schedule is no use if you are not able to carry it out due to ringing phones, colleagues stopping by, dozens of emergencies and so on.

Defending your time

There are many tips and tricks to setting up a properly productive schedule like my example above, but the first thing you must figure out is how to protect your time. This ties in with setting limits, as discussed in the second chapter. You will need to know what is important to you, your goals, and be willing to defend the time you will need to put into those tasks. The problem with time management is that many people see time as free, or lacking monetary value. There is no immediate cost for taking a meeting or phone call, for example, but you will lose productivity as a result.

One way to become a better defender of your time is to figure out what it is worth. Break down your salary by hour and keep this figure in mind when someone asks you for some time. Will it be worth whatever you earn that hour to you and/or your library to take the time? You may want to double the figure to account for benefits, the cost of building maintenance, etc. Keep this figure in mind as you work through your day. Ask yourself if you are maximising the value of your time or costing your employer or yourself (whichever is more motivational).

I will reiterate the advice to schedule tasks in your calendar as you would an appointment, as this makes it easier to defend your time. If you have set aside an hour to work on your employees' annual reviews and a colleague asks you to join a meeting during that time, it is much easier to say no if you can see what you will need to do later if you have to reschedule a more free-floating task. If you are using a group or online calendar for scheduling meetings, having the time already blocked out on your calendar can also protect it from being used in this way. The key to success with this approach is to ensure the task is small enough to accomplish during the blocked-out period, or at least make good progress toward completion.

Multitasking

There is a false belief that you cannot make the most of your time unless you are doing several different things at once. It is not enough to attend a meeting and take notes. Now attendees must bring computers to pull up documents, find information, keep on top of e-mail and contact others. Business travellers clamour for in-flight internet access and use of cell phones rather than using the time to unplug and perhaps relax.

When our attention is divided like this, there is absolutely no way that things can get done well and thoroughly in the minimum amount of time. When a person is multitasking, they are really just shifting their attention from task to task without focusing on anything for more than a few seconds. Our brains are not capable of focusing on more than one task at a time (Abaté, 2008). When your mother said you could not do your homework and watch television at the same time, she was completely right. The same principle applies to your work now. You cannot keep on top of e-mail, take phone calls, write a report and chat with a co-worker all at once. Multitasking is like catnip for procrastination. You feel as if you are getting all sorts of tasks done but in essence you are wasting time.

Yet we still feel the need to do as much at once as we think we can handle. No one wants to admit that they work best when focusing only on the task at hand. It sounds lazy in this present day, when we have 24-hour news networks and grocery shopping and our work is only a BlackBerry away. Of course, there are situations where multitasking is a blessing – see the section on smart multitasking below. But in general, when we are working on an important task, that task will get done quicker and better if we do it alone rather than in combination with another important task.

In the interest of productivity and our own sanity we must take a stand. Try just doing one thing at a time, just to see how different it feels to dedicate your entire attention and focus to the task at hand. It may be challenging at first if you are used to the interruptions. Some have likened the sensation to rewiring their brains (Jacobs, 2009). But if you try it, you will likely notice you are getting more done, better, in less time. Do not be afraid to share this productivity 'secret' with your colleagues, to combat the doctrine of multitasking.

Dealing with meetings

In most jobs, an inordinate amount of work time is taken up with meetings. In my library, at least, we cannot seem to get anything done without at least three meetings first. Meetings can be quite valuable yet they often serve little purpose. How can you make them work better?

The best thing to do is attend only those meetings with value for your work. A valuable meeting is usually short – one hour or less. If your meetings are taking longer, you may need to consider what you are trying to accomplish – would training sessions be more appropriate? Could information be shared in a less time-intensive way, say, via a memo or e-mail?

A valuable meeting will have an agenda prepared in advance. That agenda will be action-oriented and relevant to your work in some way. Information-sharing is not a reason to call a meeting. It is a waste of time to call a meeting just to inform others about library happenings. A far better way to share that information is via a memo that can be read at leisure. In the same way, all well-run meetings should produce minutes that can be read by anyone with an interest in the topic who was unable to attend. Even if the meeting is not public – for whatever reason – some record should still be kept. If not, appoint yourself (or someone else if you have the power) official note-taker and make sure these notes are made available at least to attendees and anyone absent.

Meetings should be run by people who value their time and your time, and the agenda should guide the meeting. Meetings should end on time or early – never late. To speed up your meetings, try some of the following:

- Run the meeting with everyone standing – no chairs allowed. People generally get tired of standing after about 20 minutes and this can be an excellent incentive to end the meeting.

- Keep a large clock in the room or use a projector to display the time on the wall in a very large font. If you only have a set amount of time, you might also use a countdown timer, or run a stopwatch to display how long the meeting is taking. Seeing time pass before your eyes can help you accomplish tasks faster.

- When the inevitable happens and someone goes off the agenda to bring up 'just one thing' use a whiteboard or flipchart as a 'parking lot' for these ideas. This will allow them to remain visible to all attendees, so they do not get lost in the shuffle. Write them down after the meeting, and add them to the next meeting's agenda. Do not discuss them at the current meeting. This prevents your dedicated time for a particular task from being hijacked into a discussion for which no one is prepared.

Your ability to suggest or implement these tips probably varies depending on who is running the meeting or your role in the group. It may be difficult to try some of these tips if you are not in a position of power. Try talking with whoever leads the meeting and emphasise that these tips will save everyone's valuable time. Or, to get out of a meeting entirely, try telling the meeting leader or your supervisor that you feel your time would be better spent working on a particular project and that you would like to miss the meeting 'just this once'. Do this for a few meetings and keep on top of any minutes or reports; after a while, impress the meeting leader or your supervisor with your knowledge of what happened at the meeting despite your lack of attendance and with how much work you completed in the meantime and then ask to be excluded permanently.

Maybe we are lucky enough to work somewhere with functional and valuable meetings, or somewhere we can choose whether or not to attend a meeting. However, this is probably not the case. I have worked in some places where the all-staff meetings were basically information-sharing sessions: department heads reported on projects they or their employees were carrying out, and other department heads would comment on the projects. Most of the rest of the employees had no role and very little interest in what was going on. How can we make such meetings a better use of our time? Or what can we do when we have downtime before a meeting starts, or at the doctor's office, or waiting in line for a print job?

Smart multitasking

In general, multitasking is the enemy of productivity. But in some cases it can be beneficial to work on a task while ostensibly doing something else. If you are in a meeting that does not serve much purpose, this may be a good time to draft an outline for a research project. If you are waiting for a phone call to be returned and cannot leave your office, this is a great time to get a start on those annual reviews. Dave Crenshaw (2008) calls this 'background tasking', when you are performing one or two actions that do not require decision-making or deep thinking.

This can tie with the grouping of tasks discussed in the last chapter. If you have a task that you know will involve some downtime, like waiting for a phone call or working on the reference desk, pair it with catching up on professional reading or something similar that can be easily interrupted. Do not try to do more than two things at once, otherwise things head back into 'dumb multitasking' territory. To determine whether what you are doing is smart multitasking, ask yourself if you are giving both activities the attention they merit and if you are performing at an adequate level. If not, pick the task with the higher priority and stick with it until it is done, then switch to the other task.

Office hours

In the previous chapter we discussed dealing with distractions. What if some of your distractions are your co-workers? Perhaps the people who report to you often have questions or suggestions. Perhaps you are working on a group project, but it is not your only task to complete. A possible solution to the interruptions brought up by these situations is to set up office hours.

Office hours are popular in academia. They give students and colleagues a set time to find professors in their offices, in a receptive mindset. This concept could be carried over into any library and gives those with whom you work a time that they can reach you with any needs they have, rather than interrupting you scattershot throughout the day. This does however require both sides to take the agreement seriously. You will need to be present and available during your office hours. This is something I struggle with – I have a tendency to wander off and away from my desk. Your colleagues will have to learn that this is the best time, or maybe the only time, when they can interrupt you.

If you provide your colleagues with such time, it is much easier to block out time when you cannot be interrupted.

For me, the best way to have uninterrupted time is to go home and switch off my phone and e-mail. I have tried closing my office door, only to have co-workers and students open it up and come in. I have tried locking the door, only to have them knock loudly and repeatedly. If this happens to you, the only option may be to work elsewhere! Other people may be more receptive to a discreet 'do not disturb' sign that also lists your office hours. In any case, if people are clear that there are certain times when you are available and willing to assist them, they are more likely to be respectful of any 'do not disturb' notice you put out in the meantime.

Tracking interruptions exercise

Try tracking interruptions for at least one day. Draw up two columns, with your plan for the day in the first column, and space for any interruptions in the second. Among other things, your interruptions might include:

- colleagues stopping by to chat;
- people contacting you by phone/instant messenger;
- any time in which you are distracted by e-mail or web surfing;
- times when you are multitasking more than one important task.

Setting priorities

Now that we have discussed some of the mechanics for blocking out time, how do we determine what is most important? Chapter 2, on motivation, offers excellent guidance. Chapter 3, on procrastination, also deals with setting priorities when discussing to-do lists. Take another look at your goals and your big picture, keep deadlines in mind, and figure out what needs to get done when. Put deadlines into your new calendar and stick to them.

Many people swear by assigning categories to tasks based on priorities. These categories could have labels like A, B and C, or you could get more descriptive and categorise based on goal or colour code. Using categories to help with prioritising can help you make quick decisions regarding the importance of a particular task given what it will accomplish and its deadline; knowing the relevant importance of a task helps you schedule it accordingly.

Another technique to prioritising, which originated with Stephen Covey (1989) but has been mentioned over and over in the books I have read, is to adopt two binaries: important or not important, and due soon versus not due soon. By assigning these labels to one's tasks, one obtains a scale of priority:

1. important and due soon (most important);

2. important and not due soon;

3. not important and due soon;

4. not important and not due soon (least important).

Most people give the deadline more weight than the importance of the task, but many experts suggest otherwise. It makes sense if you can pull it off. Working on the important stuff should trump deadlines, but this also depends on the consequence for missing a deadline. If all is reasonable, a not-so-important task will not suffer too much from missing a deadline, but your workplace priorities may vary.

When setting priorities and creating a schedule, it is important to have a good idea how long tasks will take to accomplish. If you were able to break your tasks into manageable chunks, as discussed in the last chapter, you will have a good idea how long those chunks take to complete and can schedule your time accordingly. It is usually a good idea to budget a little more time than you think you might need to allow extra room in case of last-minute emergencies. Be careful not to give yourself too much time, however, as it may be easier to procrastinate on a deadline that you know you can meet very easily, and you could use the time much better in other ways.

The priority of the task can also help you decide how much time and effort to spend on it. If you are creating a guide for a subject area or class that you know will only be used once and perhaps half-heartedly by a handful of students, it may not be worth your absolute best effort. Perhaps that time and energy could be spent on a more important task, like your employees' annual evaluations, which will be seen by many senior staff and reviewed closely.

When setting priorities for your time and schedule, keep in mind the things we've covered so far. When do you work best, and what types of work do you want to do when? Schedule things like checking e-mail, office hours, lunch and so on according to these preferences and workflow strengths. Fit in those tasks and deadlines around the steady commitments. Try to keep a consistent daily or weekly routine despite your changing tasks. This will help you feel more grounded and calm in what can be a very stressful environment of change, and this sense of stability can help carry you through your work day and keep you productive.

For those who are scientifically minded, there are several formulae out there to help you prioritise tasks. Pareto analysis helps you find the most important tasks to give you the biggest benefit via the 80/20 rule by the same name. Paired comparison analysis allows you to weigh a handful of very different tasks or projects against one another to decide which is the most important. Grid analysis allows you to weigh many good alternatives to determine a course of action. An action priority matrix can help you determine the impact of tasks versus their effort, allowing you to assign tasks to categories like 'quick wins', 'major projects', 'fill ins' or 'thankless tasks'. The nominal group technique can help a group of people establish priorities based on individual rankings. For more information about any of these techniques, just pick up a business management text or search for them on the internet.

Your supervisor's and organisation's priorities also weigh heavily into your calculus of priorities. If what your boss or institution thinks is important is not evident to you, you have a responsibility as a good and productive employee to seek clarification. Your boss should be able to explain why a task is important and how important it is. If not, you both need to examine why it exists.

Delegating

A key component to time management is knowing when and how to delegate. This was covered a bit in Chapter 2 and will also be addressed in Chapter 6, on managing for productivity. Once you have drafted a schedule or time management plan, you may start to see where tasks could be more effectively delegated to fit in better with your and others' workflows. Keep the components we discussed in mind – are you delegating the right task to the right person for the right reasons? What is the best way to use your time?

A challenge of delegating is to get over the feeling that you can do the task better than whoever else may be appropriate. Keep your priorities and the priorities of your workplace in mind. How important is the task to you? How important is the task to your workplace? How important is it that the task is done the way you want it done? Are you providing a good learning experience for someone else, or making sure the right person is working on the job? Delegating means giving up responsibility for the task, not just giving the work to someone else. Be sure that you do this wholeheartedly.

Although you are delegating the task completely, this does not mean you are out of the picture entirely. Keep in touch and monitor the progress of the task. Ask for status reports and see if you can be of assistance, especially if the task is new to the other person. Furthermore, be sure that you are clear about your expectations regarding the task you are delegating. Specify any deadlines, goals to be met and other relevant information and contacts, as well as any guidelines you may have for the task. Clearly define the outcome you expect and be sure the person to whom you are delegating has the necessary tools, information and authority to complete it.

Calendar tools

Now that we have discussed how to schedule and manage your time in the abstract, we can address the physical tools to help us accomplish this. A calendar external to your own memory is essential. Good productivity depends on your ability to get processes out of your head to free up that mental energy for your actual work. As with to-do lists, the main question is paper or electronic.

Paper calendars

There are hundreds of varieties of paper calendars out there: bound books with a page for each day, week or month, ranging from pocket to desk size; flat desk calendars; monthly or daily wall calendars; a plain paper notebook in which you write the dates. They have the same pros and cons as paper to-do lists. In the pro column, paper has no special tools, no learning curve and no need for electricity. Paper can be easily carried with you wherever you go. Paper can be easily changed or adjusted if you have an eraser. However, paper is not easily shared with many people, especially if changes are made frequently. Paper can also be lost. I once lost my paper day-planner and felt myself lost for weeks.

If in the last chapter you decided paper was for you, you will probably feel the same way about paper calendars. They are an excellent entry point into time management and scheduling and you can always adopt a more complex system once you have explored the basics. They are also relatively cheap, so you can try out a variety to see which format works best for you.

Electronic and online calendars

If you would like the convenience of electronic or online calendars – easy sharing, easy updating, ability to use with a device like a cell phone or computer – and are willing to put up with the potential downsides – losing electricity, memory erasure, general computer frustrations – there are also a plethora of other software and online options. Software tends to be something you download to your computer and then not need to maintain an internet connection to use. It is generally tied to the computer on which you downloaded the software. Online options usually are housed elsewhere online and are thus accessible from any computer, but do require an internet connection. Some are free and some cost money. Some are tied in with systems of productivity that we will analyse in the next chapter.

Your place of work may already provide you with a software calendar. Users of Microsoft e-mail products usually have a built-in calendar that can be shared online with co-workers. Meetings can be scheduled easily through your existing e-mail program, which will show you who is available when. This has the upside of fitting in well with an existing workflow, plus most of your colleagues will be using the same tool and you can likely create group schedules or compatible individual schedules. However, it may be hard to configure the calendar to display in a way you can use easily. I end up printing out or rewriting the calendar every week, hanging it next to my computer so that I don't have to open up my e-mail every time I want to see what's on my calendar.

Some webmail providers, such as Google and Yahoo, also offer an excellent calendar service. Indeed, I prefer the Google calendar to most others I have seen, including the Microsoft one I use through work. The Google calendar is easy to share with others and is not dependent on their use of the service. It is also easy to configure with colours and labels, and offers a number of applications that allow it to display on your desktop or in other software that may be more easily incorporated into your workspace or workflow.

A blended approach

My personal favourite time management tool is a hybrid option. I keep my main calendar online in my Google account. This allows me to easily access the information from any computer as well as from some of my wireless devices, including my cell phone. I can share the calendar very easily with my husband and with my students, with differing levels of privacy. My husband's calendar is incorporated into mine so I can see at a glance what he has scheduled.

As I mentioned, I am required by my place of work to use Microsoft Outlook/Entourage. For a while I had a software patch that allowed for easy synching between Google and Microsoft, but this no longer works. As such, I am currently forced to keep two calendars up to date in order to meet my workplace obligations and keep information in a format that is convenient to me. It is not too onerous to double-check once a week to make sure events are scheduled in both places, but I still look for a synching solution.

In addition, I keep my schedule for the next two to four weeks printed out and clipped next to my computer monitor. I use the printable CEO templates mentioned in the previous chapter (*http://davidseah.com/blog/the-printable-ceo-series/*) and am thus able to incorporate my to-do list, major weekly goals, meetings, deadlines and weekly-review documents together in one spot. At the end of each week, I file my print schedule in my tenure catch-all folder for subsequent review. In this way I can simply grab my print schedule off the wall and without opening a program see if I have time for a meeting or project in the next few weeks. I can also take this plan with me to meetings or outside the office for better planning. I just have to remember to transfer over any new meetings or dates to my electronic schedules.

It took me about two years to find a solution that worked for me and it is still a work in progress. I would love to get rid of the Microsoft software requirement and maintain my schedule solely on Google, but must admit that Outlook/ Entourage provides a convenient way to coordinate my schedule with my colleagues' schedules, although it is definitely not an *easy* way to do so.

Not just the tools

Even though I have a system of time management figured out, good time management requires far more than a calendar.

You must maintain a commitment to yourself, to honour your agreements with and responsibilities to others and your own goals. My time would not be well managed if I did not account for most of my actions and tasks, block them out on my calendar and actually carry through and work on them when I plan to do so. Again, productivity comes down to an honest desire for change and to change. Once I committed to this, I started reaping the rewards – getting things done quickly and efficiently, knowing what I was going to work on when, with less anxiety and more time for myself. It is not easy to stick with this commitment at times, but if I slip up for a few days, I am soon reminded how much more difficult life can be without time management.

Productivity is a lot like dieting. You cannot carry out a productive work life at all times, but it improves life immensely when you do. In addition, much like dieting, it can help to follow a proscribed system, as will be explored in the next chapter.

Questions to consider

- Effective scheduling and time management is dependent on the ability to say no and set priorities. Will you need to work on this area in order to succeed?

- How will using a physical calendar and scheduling help you most? Is your main need to keep on track with tasks or to avoid disruptions and procrastination? Are you missing important appointments?

- Do you have existing software or workflows that can be adapted into a scheduling tool? Do you have a mandated tool you will have to use?

5

Systems of productivity

Instituting changes to improve your life sometimes works more smoothly when there is a structured or organised way to do so. In the last chapter, I mentioned diets as an example. We all know that losing weight and maintaining health means eating right and exercising, but when we begin down that path it can be helpful to have an outline of what to eat when, how much to eat, how much exercise to get, and so on. Most diet books and plans are really a system of eating right and exercising.

There are a number of productivity systems that can provide us with that same kick-start. They can guide us into making better choices about how we spend our time and plan our days. They can provide us with the framework that eases us into using our time and energies more efficiently. They can make some of the hard decisions easier.

Systems have generally been created by experts (or at least people who perceive themselves as experts) to deal with problems in a consistent and coherent manner. Adopting a system can give you a set of productivity tools that work well together and make logical sense. The systems that reach publication and become relatively well known have been tried and tested as well. They are popular because there is something about them that works.

Trying out a system of productivity can get you thinking about your workflow in a new way. This book thus far has been introspective – analysing why you do what you do and how to best work with your habits and tendencies. Systems question you on why you have these tendencies in the first place and suggest complementary activities or wholesale replacements.

Another thing a system can do for you is minimise the number of choices you have to make. By relegating your actions to a few different choices, it becomes much easier to make good decisions about how to spend your time. Diets apply this same principle. If the types of food you eat are restricted in some way, it makes it easier for you to decide what to eat, and to make this decision within a healthier context. Although systems and diets restrict you in some ways, there is still room in both for personal choice and needs.

This chapter will review seven of the major recent productivity systems: the Seven Habits series, Getting Things Done, Never Check E-mail in the Morning, Bit Literacy, the Four-Hour Workweek, Zen to Done, and One Year to an Organized Work Life. After a short discussion of each, I will compare and contrast the seven and offer some suggestions on how to choose a system, should you want the guidance and organisation that is provided by one.

The Seven Habits of Highly Effective People

As we discussed back in the first chapter, personal productivity began to be studied early in the twentieth century. However, one of the first true systems of productivity was introduced in 1989 with the publication of Stephen Covey's *The Seven Habits of Highly Effective People*. The book was an instant hit and remains popular to the present day, spawning several more books by the author, training sessions and seminars, products such as the FranklinCovey day-planners, software and more.

The original book has a chapter dedicated to each of the seven habits. Each habit is defined and the author discusses his experiences with implementing the habit in his life and how others have implemented it along with their reactions. Along with these parables, he offers direct suggestions for implementing the habit in your own life, further illustrating points with tables, charts and graphs.

The seven habits, which are explained more fully below, are:

- be proactive;
- begin with the end in mind;
- put first things first;
- think win-win;
- seek first to understand, then to be understood;
- synergise;
- sharpen the saw.

The habits build upon one another to lead the individual from dependence to independence to interdependence. The first three habits are seen as creating a 'private victory' while the next three create a 'public victory'. The final habit circles and embodies the previous six. A diagram is used to represent this structure throughout the book. Each chapter ends with exercises to apply the habit to your thinking and way of life.

The first habit of proactivity is fairly self-explanatory. The chapter aims to break the stimulus-response cycle that traps many of us into a workflow where crises occur and we react. It points out that proactive people exercise their freedom to choose how to react to stimuli in a thoughtful and responsible way. We can take the initiative to shape our lives in a particular way. The author suggests taking 30 days to just 'be' and work on what you can control.

Habit two – begin with the end in mind – is an exploration of goal-setting. Keeping your goals in mind as you work or live life allows you to make more mindful choices. The author walks the reader through creating a personal mission statement and identifying their principles.

Putting first things first is the third habit and deals with prioritising. The author presents a matrix of time management to help the reader shape priorities. This chapter also has excellent tips on how to turn down requests for time.

Habit four – think win-win – deals with fostering a belief in a positive outcome for everyone involved in a situation. It focuses on five dimensions: character, relationships, agreements, supportive systems and processes. This chapter is the root of the abundance mentality that I discussed previously when dealing with motivation.

Seek first to understand, then to be understood, is the fifth habit and valuable personal advice. This chapter deals with effective interpersonal communication and contains the time-honoured 'restate the statement and reflect the meaning' technique of empathic listening.

Synergise, the sixth habit, means that combining the parts discussed so far in the book will lead to an even greater whole, in that the parts build upon each other in creative and fulfilling ways. The section has useful tips for dealing with change and disagreement in a positive manner.

The seventh and final habit, sharpen the saw, is subtitled 'principles of balanced self-renewal'. This handy chapter helps deal with those who may fall off the wagon of the system and deals well with issues of work-life balance.

In addition to the habits-oriented chapters, Covey spends considerable time discussing the need to change one's personal paradigms for attitude and behaviours. He talks about seeing things 'inside-out' to get a new and better perspective on tough situations. According to Covey's way of thinking, responsibility for problems is firmly rooted with the individual.

Covey's books call for a total revolution in how you think about work and life. He writes from a values-oriented perspective and has a genuine aim to improve the reader's life all around. The content does lean more toward the self-help books of the 1970s and 1980s, but with its practical advice for implementing the habits, it moves toward the more action-oriented works of the 1990s and 2000s. The third habit, putting first things first, deals most explicitly with time management and productivity. Future books by Covey expand more on time management themes.

One of the more enduring examples from his book is a particular visualisation. Imagine your goals are big rocks. The major tasks you want to complete are little rocks. All the other little things you must do are sand. Now you must fit all these items into a bucket, which symbolises your life. If you do not start with the big rocks and work your way down, the sand will take up too much space and you will not have room for all the rock. With the larger rocks serving as the foundation, however, the sand can easily slip in the gaps.

As the longest-lasting book on productivity, there has been some academic study and application of the habits to various disciplines. Primarily the fields of organisational and social psychology and sociology have looked at the phenomenon, but the occasional professional journal has adapted the habits to their discipline, in article form. These are listed in the final chapter on further resources.

Getting Things Done

David Allen's *Getting Things Done: The Art of Stress-Free Productivity* was first published in 2001. This book took productivity out of the 'self-help' arena and made it more approachable for the average person. The key to the *Getting Things Done* system is to move tasks, appointments and other information outside your head and record them externally. The book offers three models for doing this: a workflow process, a framework with six levels of focus, and a planning method. The key question, to be asked at nearly every turn, is 'What's the next action?' Another hallmark of the system is to control the inputs of information into your life – consolidate information into one 'inbox' for processing. It is, true to its name, focused on getting things done.

Getting Things Done takes a step away from the 'values' approach that *Seven Habits* established as the key to productivity and deals more with creating a 'productive state', where a worker works effortlessly and with focus on the tasks at hand. Compared with *Seven Habits*, and in fact with most productivity books, *Getting Things Done* can be rather dry, more like a software manual than a guidebook for personal change. Along with taking a practical and non-self-help approach, *Getting Things Done* was one of the first productivity systems to deal with the rise of the internet and the 'always on' culture that has been brought into and out of the workplace, with e-mail, BlackBerrys, 24/7 access to the web and other developments.

The book is not as visually-oriented as *Seven Habits* but does include a few flow-charts to outline the processes of the system. There are no set exercises in the vein of *Seven Habits*, but the structure of the book is such that you are encouraged to follow it along and thus enact Allen's system. The first half of the book provides an outline for getting your life organised and under control quickly and sets up the core principles of *Getting Things Done*, which are:

- collect;
- process;
- organise;
- review;
- do.

Collect focuses on the various inputs your work life might have: e-mail, phone messages, appointments, paper mail, etc. The author recommends creating one central inbox to manage all of the 'stuff' associated with work in the twenty-first century. *Process* is described as 'getting "in" to empty' and deals with what to do with all that stuff you collected. It is a true workflow in that it goes in only one direction, never back to 'in'. *Organise* is fairly self-explanatory and talks about setting up 'buckets' for your stuff and makes the claim that 'all you really need is lists and folders' (Allen, 2001: 140). *Review* deals with keeping your system functional and on task by periodically reviewing goals, calendars and to-do lists. *Do* is also another self-evident principle, with the author setting up three models for 'making action choices' (Allen, 2001: 48).

The second part expands on this first part with more detail and methodology, while the third part of the book explores why this system works and what can be gained from this approach. Much emphasis is put on the importance of planning in these final chapters, and the author demonstrates that planning and following through on the system can drastically benefit productivity, self-esteem, relaxation, empowerment and outcomes.

Concrete and systematic review is one of the book's key contributions to the productivity field. At nearly every step of the system, a review process is built in. This keeps individuals on task and focused on goals in a way that *Seven Habits* does not. Planning and review happen on both the horizontal level, going into the future and looking at the past, and also on the vertical, with overarching professional goals, weekly goals, annual objectives and more coming into play. Allen insists that 'front-end planning', i.e. doing as much thinking in advance of acting as possible, reduces stress and creates a better and more productive work environment.

One of my favourite suggestions from Allen's book is the tickler file. Take a simple accordion file and add 43 folders. Label a folder for each month, and label the rest 1–31. File away information for future months in the appropriate folder, then parcel out the information for the current month by day. Agendas for meetings, information for reports, and reminders to perform tasks can be parcelled out over the year, and all one needs to do is pull out the appropriate folder.

Getting Things Done has approached cult status in the past decade and has spawned nearly as many spin-off products as Covey's works, including diaries, notepaper, software, courses and further books. However, many followers find it difficult to adhere strictly to the full level of detail to which the system goes. Even the author has admitted he does not follow the system perfectly. Due to its complexity, I have not adapted the *Getting Things Done* method to my own work situation, but instead have taken parts of the workflow process and adapted them to how I work best. I endeavour to keep tasks and information coming in to one central inbox, have set up a tickler file, and have also incorporated parts of the various review processes into my schedule.

Never Check E-Mail in the Morning

In 2004, Julie Morgenstern's *Making Work Work* was rereleased as *Never Check E-Mail in the Morning*. Coming on the coattails of *Getting Things Done*, Morgenstern also had the backing of Oprah Winfrey and this led to a bit of publicity for her work. Her focus is on finding happiness in your work rather than increasing productivity as such, but her method still serves as a rough system for us to examine.

Her book has less of a structure compared with the others examined. It begins with an examination of the reader as a worker, claiming that employees fall into three tiers. The majority of workers, she claims, are in the middle tier. They do reliable work, and although they make the occasional mistake, they are generally good workers and get the job done. The underperformers that drag down the organisation make up the bottom tier, while the organisation's star performers make up the top tier. The book contains a quiz so you can identify the tier to which you belong – I was pleased to see I place in the top tier, although just barely.

The rest of the book is divided into nine 'competencies':

- embrace your work-life balance;
- develop an entrepreneurial mindset;
- choose the most important tasks;
- create the time to get things done;
- control the nibblers;
- organise at the speed of change;
- master delegation;
- work well with others;
- leverage your value.

Most of these sections are pretty self-explanatory. 'Control the nibblers' deals with the various time-wasters a worker might face, such as perfectionism, procrastination, physical interruptions and meetings. 'Leverage your value' discusses how to make the most of the 'new and improved' you, as regards seeking raises or more challenging work.

This book has a definite business/managerial bent and hearkens back to the values approach of *Seven Habits*. Sidebars illustrate points from the book with personal stories, usually from female managers. Chapters include quizzes and 'grab and go' strategies that are designed for immediate implementation into your workday. They end with a summary of important points and questions to consider. Chapters also contain examples of situations with the question, 'Is it me or is it them?' with practical suggestions on how to tell if the obstacle is you or your workplace, and how to deal with the problem either way.

Morgenstern's book is definitely targeted at women; indeed, it is the one of the few books on productivity written by a woman that I came across in my research, which adds a new perspective. It is written in a personable, conversational manner and strives to deal with issues of insecurity, anxiety and stress more directly than any other work that I examined. Despite this, or maybe because of this, it deals with issues of financial value in the workplace better than any other book I read, perhaps because there is no assumption that the reader knows about business concepts. The chapter on controlling the nibblers had excellent tips on how to say no, which is also seen as more of a 'female' concern.

As you can guess from the book's title, the key tip is not to check your e-mail as soon as you get to work but instead wait an hour and use the time when you first get to work for your most critical task of the day. This tip is reiterated by several other productivity experts. Morgenstern argues that waiting to check e-mail and using that early morning time to reach an important goal allows you to focus better and perform well on your most crucial tasks. This will also fuel your sense of accomplishment for the day. Not checking your e-mail for at least an hour allows you to break the cycle of procrastination and crisis reaction into which many of us settle.

My favourite chapter is on creating time, as a choice phrase of mine is 'you can't make time'. I was thus curious how the author would suggest this was possible. The chapter mostly deals with time management and contains helpful hints on prioritising and scheduling. The suggestion I love most is the office-wide 'quiet hour', where workers take their phones off the hook, turn off e-mail and avoid interrupting one another. Not very practical for libraries, but an intriguing idea nonetheless – especially given that one workplace she describes announces its daily quiet hour by sounding a gong!

Bit Literacy

Mark Hurst's *Bit Literacy* was released in 2007. It applies productivity tactics directly to the information age. Dealing primarily with e-mail and information overload, *Bit Literacy* offers a strategy for dealing with tools of the trade for knowledge workers and the work is directly applicable to what library workers encounter on a day-to-day basis. The short book presents techniques for managing all the bits of information that flood into our work lives. Its starting point, working your way to and maintaining an empty e-mail inbox, has bloomed into the 'Inbox Zero' movement. I attempt to maintain an empty e-mail inbox, acting on, passing along, or filing away e-mails as I read them, and it has been a great boon to my productivity. Colleagues are shocked to hear that I tend to spend no more than an hour on e-mail each day. It is amazing how much time and energy this frees up, and for good reason, tips on reducing and consolidating e-mail take up about a third of the book.

The book also offers tips on creating a bit-literate to-do list. While serving as an ad for software available from the author, it does make salient points about the need to manage your to-do list well over time. There is an interesting discussion on the lifecycle of a to-do task – tasks do not always show up on your to-do list as they need to be done. Some tasks need to incubate before they are acted upon, or need to be performed on a regular schedule; electronic files and software may be a better way to manage these with built-in reminders that are incorporated into your workflow.

Organising electronic files and file-naming conventions are also discussed in detail, as well as the management of files and information in general. A phrase pops up repeatedly – 'let the bits go'. What the author means by this is that we must mindfully reorganise, reschedule and even delete information. E-mail in particular is not meant to last forever. This book will make you feel OK about using the delete button on your e-mail, and not saving every set of meeting minutes you ever produced.

Another chapter is devoted to reducing information overload by going on a 'media diet', a concept this book covers in depth in Chapter 7. Hurst asks you to consider whether what you read is worth your time and proposes that much of our tension comes from our desire to feel constantly informed. This certainly describes a lot of library workers that I know. Our profession leads us to feel like we must know everything about everything. But of course we cannot. Hurst suggests that we do not even try, but instead become more mindful of the media we consume and their effect on our stress levels and time as well as our knowledge.

This book is definitely targeted at those who work with computers and want to do so, although it is written for those who do not understand them and are not tech-savvy. It can be incredibly helpful for getting all your electronic 'bits' into place, but if you prefer organising via paper tools, this book will leave you behind.

The Four-Hour Workweek

In 2007, self-described 'serial entrepreneur and ultravagabond' Timothy Ferriss published *The Four-Hour Workweek: Escape 9–5, Live Anywhere, and Join the New Rich*. The eye-catching title is meant to attract those tired of the typical workplace grind and is best for people interested in thinking outside the box.

That said, the book does offer a number of thought-provoking tips and tricks. It has a very thorough introduction to the concept of a four-hour workweek. It involves the 'new rich' – those who harness technology to get work done in record time and shape their lives via lifestyle design, which is in essence the setting of goals and use of productivity techniques to manage time and activities. The book is structured into four steps that together form the acronym DEAL:

1. definition;
2. elimination;
3. automation;
4. liberation.

Definition means to know what you want and what you value. *Elimination* means to get rid of everything that is not what you want or value. *Automation* means finding other ways of completing onerous tasks. *Liberation* means escaping from the 40-hour working week and doing what you love.

Each section contains chapters with examples from the author's colourful life. These chapters are all capped off with a questions and actions section to help you implement the key ideas into your workflow. The book also contains hidden 'Easter eggs' that you can use to unlock online chapters on how to make money using online businesses.

This book is immensely popular among some technology-minded, entrepreneurial types, but what does it offer for library workers? The key tip that is applicable to us is to outsource any work that another entity could do more efficiently. Outsourcing work is something libraries can probably do more, but there are definite cultural and professional concerns about it. Just do a quick search of the literature or even just the internet to find pro and con arguments about outsourcing cataloguing, virtual reference services, and more. From this book's perspective, we are worrying needlessly about an option that could save us valuable time and money.

The other main idea is to know the rules of the game, whatever game that may be, and look for loopholes. This outside-the-box thinking can be incredibly valuable for most of us. In the library world, we tend to fear change and get stuck doing things the way they have always been done. An outside-the-box approach can get us over both of these hurdles.

At first, the author seems a little too outside-the-box. His personal perspective can sometimes be a bit bombastic. However, after a few chapters he settles down, offering advice and exercises that are of definite value to our profession. There are many positive visualisation and goal-setting exercises that would be use to many of us, along with exercises on breaking out of our comfort zones.

One of the more interesting sections is on the end of time management, and basically instructs readers to focus their work on situations that are profitable and easy to work with. The questions and actions in this chapter are definitely helpful in setting priorities and proposing action. The following section on the 'low information diet' is intriguing as well. The author suggests readers simply stop following the news, arguing that if a situation is important enough, you will hear about it. He also recommends cultivating a set of trusted advisers to answer questions. Of course, as librarians we are often the ones to answer these questions, so adopting the low-information diet may not be for us. Nonetheless, it may behoove us to rethink our stance that we must know everything about everything. As the author points out, not following the news frees up a large amount of time, and lowers stress significantly.

The final two sections on automation and liberation may not offer library workers much food for thought. Realistically, only so much of what we do can be automated, or so we hope, and it is probably not likely that we can put in only four hours a week at our jobs the way they are structured. However, if I am wrong about this, I would very much love to hear!

Zen to Done

Self-published as an e-book in 2008 by popular productivity blogger Leo Babauta, *Zen to Done* offers a simplified version of a productivity system based heavily on *Getting Things Done*. He offers tips on how to develop habits, then follows a structure very similar to the *Seven Habits*, with a chapter for each. Babauta's habits are:

- collect;
- process;
- plan;
- do;

- simple trusted system;
- organise;
- review;
- simplify;
- routine;
- find your passion.

Babauta also offers a chapter on 'minimal ZTD' that offers a system incorporating only the first four habits. Habits are defined, discussed with examples from the author's life, and strategies for implementation are offered. Most of these are action words and the book is heavy on action. Babauta's biggest criticism of *Getting Things Done* was that there was not enough discussion of how to take action. This book definitely addresses the *how* of getting things done.

Some of the chapters ('Collect', 'Process', 'Organise', 'Review', 'Do') are essentially the same as *Getting Things Done*. The steps are simplified, however, and some new ones are added, along with different tips for implementation. For example, 'Collect' includes the tip to always carry a notebook; 'Planning' is expanded into a habit; and 'Do' contains advice on how to get started along with tips for defeating procrastination and perfectionism. The simple trusted system habit deals with the creation of a personalised, flexible system for managing time and tasks. The simplify habit is very helpful for eliminating unnecessary or unwanted distractions, tasks and chores from your life. Setting routines is an important part of creating habits that is overlooked by most other writers. The last habit, which concerns finding your passion, is the one the author claims is most essential. As we discussed in the motivation chapter of this book, motivation can help with every aspect of productivity.

The book is just under 90 pages long and is all text – no diagrams. There are a few forms at the end of the book that can be printed out and used. Although it is only available as an e-book, it has nevertheless managed to enter the discussion of productivity. The author's blog was listed in *Time* magazine's top 25 blogs in February 2009. He has also recently released a more traditional print book from a major publisher, *The Power of Less*, which has been a best-seller on Amazon since its release.

This system has been the easiest for me to adopt. I enjoy the flexibility the author brings to adopt just part of his system as well as his introductory chapter explaining how best to make the changes required for each habit. He realises that habits do not form overnight and that gradual work toward a goal is perhaps more valuable, and more likely to stick, than a radical overhaul of how you work.

One Year to an Organized Work Life

In *One Year to an Organized Work Life: From Your Desk to Your Deadlines, the Week-by-Week Guide to Eliminating Office Stress for Good*, published in 2009, self-proclaimed 'Zen organiser' Regina Leeds turns her attention to the world of work. Leeds works as an organising consultant and has previously published a book on personal organising. This new book, focused on the workplace, has not yet received much acclaim or examination on the productivity blogosphere, but is worth examination as a system to follow.

Leeds sets up a weekly approach to becoming more organised and productive. She begins with an introduction to her philosophy of Zen organising, which essentially is about calming stress and the idea that your external environment affects the energies of your entire person. Before diving into the programme, the author advises the reader to start eating healthily and to exercise and meditate daily. She also recommends starting a productivity journal, which she mentions in exercises throughout the book, and creating a 'dream board' to help you visualise your ideal work life. What follows in her book is a week-by-week outline for an entire year's revamping of work and life organisation and productivity.

Chapters are organised by month, with a theme for each month and a work and home habit to develop throughout the month. For each week of the month there is an activity to help incorporate and practise the habits of the month. The themes are:

- start fresh;
- make the most of your office space;
- stop paper pileups;
- break your worst time-wasting habits;
- set priorities;
- how to deal with people;
- take a vacation;
- organise your virtual world;
- fine-tune for fall;
- ease business travel;
- move forward;
- balance your work and your life.

To illustrate the habits I offer an example from the first month. The home habit is to make your bed every day. The work habit is to leave your desk, take short five-minute breaks for exercise throughout the day and leave your work *at work* at the end of the day and on weekends. The weekly assignments for this month are:

- chart the course (analyse where you are now in your life and career);
- decide where you want to be (set goals);
- keep a calendar;
- calm the morning rush.

The first two assignments involve writing in a journal and the other two are fairly straightforward activities, common to nearly every productivity book we have examined. Each month's chapter ends with a short review of activities and lessons discussed before the next month begins.

While these themes are presented for a calendar year, January through December, you can start the programme at any time of year. Lessons build on one another, however, so you should still work through the book in the order presented rather than match the chapter to the month in which you begin reading. This book is fairly low-tech and mostly deals with paper resources (calendars, files, etc.), although the virtual space month deals with e-mail and computer files.

A key theme, presented in week two of February, is the 'magic formula'. This is the way to form order out of chaos and it is presented in three steps. The first is to *eliminate*. This means to remove anything no longer needed, used or desired. The second is to *categorise* whatever remains, into groupings that make sense based on the environment and tasks at hand. The final step is the *physical organisation*; the arranging of the categories into a logical and attractive whole. The particular assignment of the week in which the magic formula is introduced is to organise your desk, but the formula comes up repeatedly after this week.

As one of the few books written by a woman, there is a strong emphasis on work-life balance and the needs of working parents. The author also adopts a strongly holistic approach. While the book is ostensibly about work productivity, habits for the home are offered each month and lessons discuss work-life balance and improving productivity at home alongside work. This is an approach I value as well and one that is now becoming popular in the productivity literature.

The book's approach to taking an entire year to become more productive, with weekly assignments and monthly habits to develop, provides a strong structure to those who may have problems with an entirely new system being thrust upon them. This gradual approach allows for habits to develop naturally, leading to more lasting results. This book would be best for those who struggle with organisation above all else, as you may guess from the title. The book does not provide much guidance with higher-level thinking and planning, but it may be more important for some readers to get the basic organisation of their workplace set before they can turn to more esoteric work concerns like planning for the future.

Systems quiz

Confused or unsure if a particular system is right for you? Table 5.1 presents a quiz to figure out if you have a leaning toward one or another. Using a scale of 1 to 5, where 1 means you disagree totally and 5 means you agree completely, circle how much you agree with the statements in the table.

As you can probably guess, the quiz provides a not-so-cleverly veiled description of each system. Whichever one

Table 5.1 Productivity systems quiz

Part 1					
1) I am values-driven	1	2	3	4	5
2) I am a visual learner	1	2	3	4	5
3) Increasing my productivity will make me a better person	1	2	3	4	5
4) To become more productive I need to change my world view	1	2	3	4	5
Total for Part 1:					
Part 2					
1) I am results-driven	1	2	3	4	5
2) I am or want to be organised	1	2	3	4	5
3) I feel I am overwhelmed by requests for my time	1	2	3	4	5
4) I need a radical overhaul in how I manage my time	1	2	3	4	5
Total for Part 2:					
Part 3					
1) I am female and/or watch *Oprah*	1	2	3	4	5
2) I need a better understanding of how the business world works	1	2	3	4	5
3) I don't feel the need to change drastically	1	2	3	4	5
4) I would appreciate a career or life coach	1	2	3	4	5
Total for Part 3:					
Part 4					
1) Most of my work is done with computers	1	2	3	4	5
2) I am a victim of information overload	1	2	3	4	5
3) I prefer to work with computers vs. paper	1	2	3	4	5
4) I need tips that I can implement immediately	1	2	3	4	5
Total for Part 4:					

Table 5.1   Productivity systems quiz (*Cont'd*)

Part 5					
1) I want to minimise the amount of time that I work	1	2	3	4	5
2) I like to find creative solutions to problems	1	2	3	4	5
3) I want to radically change my workday	1	2	3	4	5
4) I want to be able to travel and set my own hours	1	2	3	4	5
Total for Part 5:					
Part 6					
1) I want to simplify my life	1	2	3	4	5
2) I like to keep the big picture in mind, and then work out details	1	2	3	4	5
3) I prefer gradual changes to big ones	1	2	3	4	5
4) I value ritual and routine	1	2	3	4	5
Total for Part 6:					
Part 7					
1) My biggest problem is organisation	1	2	3	4	5
2) I need a very strong structure to motivate me/help me stick with a programme	1	2	3	4	5
3) I am a detail person	1	2	3	4	5
4) Balance and stress-reduction are most important to me	1	2	3	4	5
Total for Part 7:					

you rate with the highest score is likely the most compatible with your mindset and current position. That said, the systems all have worthwhile suggestions and borrow from one another. I would recommend checking out a few of them to see if their structures and suggestions have anything to offer you.

A cautionary note

Remember that using a system can have downsides. For all the motivation and guidance a system provides, it can be demotivating if you fail to follow the system. Getting off-track for even a short period could sufficiently demoralise you to make you give in and return to your previous ways. The lack of simplicity and personal fit can also make it hard to stick to a system – as we learned, sometimes *Getting Things Done* does not help get things done. However, learning about these systems can help you find tools and tips for managing your workflow and becoming more productive. There is no rule that says you must adopt the whole system.

The next chapter will discuss productivity for managers, a topic we have touched upon throughout this book but one that is worthy of greater consideration. The chapter after that will stick with productivity generally. Whether or not you choose to adopt a system of productivity discussed here, the next two chapters can be a great help in keeping you going.

Questions to consider

- Thinking about your past approaches to following a system, whether a diet or some other change in habits, did you find the structure helpful, or was it more of a hindrance?

- Review your goals statements and your drafts of your ideal workday. Is there a system or two that seems to fit with how you want to shape your work? Why?

6

Managing for productivity

For most of this book I have focused on the individual's productivity, with a word here and there about supervisory duties, delegating tasks, running meetings well, and so on. Over the course of writing this book and in the course of the past year of my career, I have realised that managers have much to do with the productivity of their employees. This should come as no surprise, but what is surprising is how few managers think seriously about how to manage in a way that allows employees to produce their best efforts in the most efficient manner, despite the plethora of books and training courses on the subject. There are two key things managers must realise to truly manage for productivity. First, they must themselves be productive and efficient in their jobs, and then they must also trust their employees to be the same.

First take the mote from your own eye

We all likely have horror stories about poor managers and usually one of the defining characteristics of these stories is that the manager is not a good worker in some way, or most ways. The boss cannot type even an e-mail to save his life, does not know how to shelve a cart of books, never returns phone calls, or hides in his office when the desk is swamped. Stories about the best managers, however, usually share how they are efficient workers, understanding all basic processes of their workplace and able as well as willing to help out in any area that may need assistance with just some quick refresher training.

If you are looking to reinvent your workplace into a productive, balanced place to be, you will have to start with your own work habits. You will need to be the one that sets the example and the tone for the workplace. As silly as it may sound, your attitude and aptitude for productive work and a healthy work-life balance will do more to guide your employees to follow in your example than words ever will. So, once you have mastered the other principles in this book, how can you transfer them to your employees?

Trust is the key

The best managers I have ever had, and the ones I have learned the most from and had the most freedom to work for, were the ones who trusted their employees to do excellent work. The worst managers I have ever had, the ones for whom I did just enough to get along and meet expectations, were the ones who clearly did not trust me.

Many of the managers in the second group never allow themselves to trust their workers, because they fear their workers would abuse that trust by not working as hard. They fear a lack of control over their workers' output and effort. However, for your employees to do their best work and to feel motivated to contribute at a high level, you will need to trust them and their efforts.

Trusting employees does not mean giving them no consequences. If an employee is not giving their best efforts or even satisfactory efforts, proper disciplinary actions can and should be taken. But as we have seen, a positive workplace environment and culture can be tremendously motivating, boosting productivity and helping employees feel more invested in their jobs and responsible for their outcomes.

An excellent way to establish trust between yourself and your employees is to set clear and reasonable expectations for their work. Make sure employees have an individual job description that actually matches what they should be doing. Ensure that they understand how their jobs relate back to the library's mission and goals, and that their individual goals align with moving the library forward.

Another tactic is to involve employees in their own employment reviews. During annual reviews, ask employees to complete self-reviews in which they discuss what was most important to them about their jobs and why. This sort of self-evaluation can be incredibly insightful to you as a manager and give you important information on how to motivate your employees to do their best possible work.

Avoiding micromanagement

Nothing tells your employees that you do not trust them like micromanaging does. Most micromanagers have a hands-on attitude and a keen eye for details, which are definitely positive traits, but when taken to their extremes stifle employee problem-solving and frustrate both sides of the employment relationship. Employees feel disempowered and not trusted, while managers feel that they have to do everything in order to get things done right.

Signs of micromanaging include:

- a resistance to delegating;
- immersing yourself in overseeing the projects of others;

- correcting tiny details instead of looking at the big picture;
- taking back delegated work before it is finished if you fear an employee is making mistakes;
- discouraging others from making decisions without consulting you.

If you are caught in the trap of micromanaging, you will feel stretched too thin, time-wise. If you are overseeing everything, you will not have time to do your own work. In addition, the work you do get from your employees will not be done as well as it could be if they had the trust and empowerment to focus their full efforts on the task at hand, without interruption or fear of disapproval.

If you recognise yourself as a micromanager, you may need to learn more about delegating properly. Delegating should be planned out, with an awareness of employee workloads and skills as well as organisational priorities and other projects. Only once a plan is in place for the task, with clear objectives, actions, due dates, and a definition for successful completion, should the delegation process begin.

Be sure you choose the best person for the task, rather than the most available or easily accessible person. Confer with that person to assign the task. Discuss the measurable actions that you are requesting, the objectives of the task, what success will look like, when it is due and what kind of status reports you would like. Make sure your employee has whatever authority is needed to carry out the task. If they need to ask for particular information about budgets or get clerical support, then ensure that those things are possible. If you feel it necessary, set up a schedule for status reports.

After this point, step back from the picture. The groundwork has been laid and your employee has what they need to carry through with the task. Resist the urge to check in more than you have agreed upon – this is what your status reports should provide. When the deadline arrives or when the employee lets you know that they have finished, be sure to review the work at that point as a whole. Revisit the objectives and definition of success. Resist the urge to explain how you would have done it differently unless you truly feel it would help your employee learn something new. Keep notes on the whole process for your employee's annual review or other performance assessment.

Realise that the cure for micromanagement is not to just assign projects and step out of the picture entirely. This sudden turnaround will make you uncomfortable with the process, plus your workers will not know what to make of this dramatic change and will feel at loose ends without the continual feedback they have been conditioned to receive. Take small steps and be open and honest with your employees if possible. Let them know you recognise you have a problem with micromanaging and that they can inform you if they feel they would like to try tasks with less direct involvement from you.

If employees bring up concerns about micromanagement, it does not necessarily mean you are a micromanager – it may simply be that they do not feel trusted or empowered. Nonetheless, in the interests of your productivity and theirs, it merits concern. Put some effort into investigating how you work with your people, especially as regards communication with your employees.

Communication is everything

As discussed previously, good communication is really the only way to meet your goals, set proper limits and delegate effectively. To improve communication, you must first be honest with yourself. If you know you have problems communicating clearly with others, you will have problems being a manager and even more problems fostering a productive work environment. There are many workshops, books and courses that can help you learn better communication techniques, and I recommend them for anyone. There is almost always something of value in learning more about communication. I specifically recommend Dale Carnegie's *How to Win Friends and Influence People*, particularly Part Four, 'Be a leader: how to change people without giving offence or arousing resentment'.

The most effective communications between management and employees happen in workplaces with a culture of trust and shared responsibility, as discussed above. You as a manager play a crucial role in establishing this environment. If it is lacking, it is your job to create it. You need to build proper communication and respect along with appreciation for your employees and your library's mission. This will take time to grow, but once it is in place it will benefit the organisation and productivity overall. Recognising the importance of communication to your organisation and placing a priority on good communication will demonstrate the importance of the issue to your staff.

Communications quiz

The following quiz will help you begin thinking about how you communicate with your employees and where potential problems may lie.

1) When my employees have something to tell me:
    a) They make an appointment to talk with me
    b) They send me an e-mail

    c) They can stop by anytime or call

    d) They don't have to tell me anything – I already know what's going on

2) When I have information to share with my employees:

    a) I schedule a meeting

    b) I send an e-mail

    c) I stop by their workspaces individually

    d) I share it at the regularly scheduled meeting

3) When I have especially sensitive information to share with my employees:

    a) I schedule individual or group meetings

    b) I send an e-mail

    c) I stop by their workspaces individually

    d) I share it at the regularly scheduled meeting

4) When I have especially complex information to share with my employees:

    a) I call a special meeting

    b) I send it over e-mail

    c) I stop by their workspaces individually

    d) I share it at the regularly scheduled meeting

5) When sharing complex information:

    a) I tell my employees only what they need to know to function

    b) I tell my employees the full situation and give them context as to the implications for them as well as the organisation

In general there are no strictly right or wrong answers here, except for number 5, which we will discuss in a moment. Employers and employees have different communication styles. However, I believe that to communicate in a way that promotes a productive workplace, managers ought to consider the venue for communication, the type of information to be shared, and how their employees prefer to receive information. I have worked for places where the management communicates in one particular way, and employees are told that they are the ones who must adjust because they are not the managers. This is true, but if you are a manager concerned with productivity and good communication, this may not be the best way to get there.

As for the last question, many managers feel that giving too much information to employees can be harmful or confusing and choose to tell employees only what they need to know to do their jobs properly. However, to establish an atmosphere of open communication and trust, it is much better to provide employees with a full picture of complex information and events. If you are reorganising a department, remember that communicating the reasons behind the reorganisation, the predicted fallout and rearrangement, and your expectations to the group as a whole will facilitate better communication and trust than if you communicate only the specific information needed to carry out business as usual.

Placing regular tasks and work in context – not just complex information – will help your employees and your communication overall. If employees know why they are working on something, that knowledge will generate interest and open a dialogue that can potentially lead to more improvements in workflow processes. When tasks are framed in context, employees and managers can also explore options for developing skills or sharing information outside the workplace such as at a conference. Taking a lifelong learning approach with your employees and their tasks will make their work more interesting for all involved and increase commitment and productivity.

Availability

Interacting with employees is one of the biggest consumers of managers' time. Some books estimate that this takes up 50–80 per cent of a manager's workday. This does not need to be the case. Open and trustful communication can be established between managers and employees without the manager giving up quite so much time.

The previously discussed tip of holding office hours can be applied to those you manage. Set up a few hours a week to adopt an 'open door' policy where your employees can come by or call to chat about any concern. This can also work to eliminate interruptions and you can feel better about closing your office door in the interim to get work done, knowing that employees have a set time to discuss issues. The frequency and time you spend doing this is completely adjustable. For example, if employees are used to interrupting you at will, you might start with a daily open door hour. Once they get used to the idea of a set time to interact, you could cut out days, set up a block of time once or twice a week, or whatever works out well for you and your employees.

A related concept is to hold a regular individual meeting with those who report to you, weekly, monthly, or however often is needed. I personally hate regularly scheduled one-to-one meetings; for me they represent an excessive reporting commitment when I would rather have my employees come by (within office hours) as situations arise or ideas occur to them. However, if you manage at a higher level than I do, regular one-to-ones can be invaluable for getting progress reports on tasks and projects and giving feedback, context and suggestions in a timely manner.

You will of course need provisions for communicating with employees in case of emergency or unusual circumstances outside these scheduled times. Unfortunately, many of us fall into the trap of crisis management rather than managing our time well.

Breaking the cycle of crisis management

In general, work in your library should be routine. Materials come in and go out, people ask reference questions, and items are catalogued. Crisis management should be limited to emergencies – situations that cannot be predicted or prevented, such as a flu outbreak or a flood. Regular situations that can be predicted or prevented should not merit the same treatment.

Consider the example of a delayed shipment of new books. Usually this is only a small blip in the life of a library. Maybe a manager would be notified, just to be kept in the loop and be able to plan for a potential backlog. However, if the arrival of the late shipment caused a sort of crisis, where employees were not sure how to deal with the sudden (to them) heavy workload, this could cause some excitement. Such excitement can be rewarding as the job just gets more interesting. How will all these books get out on the shelf? How will we ever catch up? Dealing with these issues can then delay regularly scheduled tasks, creating more crises and yet more excitement. Going from crisis to crisis, people become reactive and further perpetuate the cycle.

We discussed this a bit in Chapter 3 on procrastination. Some people thrive on an exciting work environment and prefer to operate from a crisis mode to get that thrill. However, it is not beneficial to other employees who are also stuck in this feeling of crisis, and productivity obviously suffers. It is much healthier and more advantageous to arrest crisis management before it turns into a cycle.

The first step in dealing with crisis management is to identify that it is a problem and also identify where and how it comes up. Is it an individual? Is it the climate of the workplace? If an individual thrives on crisis, this must be dealt with quickly to avoid becoming part of the workplace climate. Once ingrained in the organisation's everyday work and workflows, crisis management becomes increasingly difficult to root out.

The second step is to realise that the situation is not truly a crisis. If something can be predicted or prevented, then it should be predicted or prevented. What stopped this from happening? Who should have caught it and where? Analyse communication structures to see what fell apart. Make sure that crisis management is not becoming the status quo, that individuals and the group can recognise what is a crisis and what is preventable.

The most important step is to stop getting caught up in the thrill and emotion of crisis management. Defuse the situation, and work on improving communications and workflow to predict or prevent situations from happening in the future. Be sure not to reward the individuals or the climate that promotes crisis management. Sometimes we praise those who have dealt with the problem rather than those who work to prevent the situation in the future.

Burnout and the organisation

Earlier in this book I addressed burnout and the individual, sharing some steps to combat this problem on a personal level. I alluded to the fact that burnout can be induced by the organisation in which you work. Factors such as micromanagement, constant crisis management, and the wrong level of management availability can hasten burnout. And, of course, burnout on the managerial level will affect the organisation to a high degree.

Feeling ineffectual can particularly contribute to burnout and is something that the management of an organisation can control. This goes hand in hand with communication as discussed above. If your employees know their role in the organisation and know how that role contributes to the organisation's success, this knowledge can help prevent their burnout and related problems. Be sure that employees do have the power to act within their roles – check for micromanagement or other barriers to prevent your employee, who knows his or her job and how it contributes to the library, from feeling like he or she cannot do their job.

Some have said that the antidote to burnout is engagement. Again, improved communication can help your employees become more engaged as they see the value of their role and what they contribute. Engagement does depend on the individual in many ways, but it is clearly something that management can facilitate and, for the purposes of productivity, ought to facilitate.

What other steps can you take if you are in a workplace where burnout is a factor? Analyse the job duties of any employees you view as at risk of burnout. Are they fair? Do employees know what they are getting into when they take on new roles or tasks? What kind of training could help employees with their work tasks? Could the whole organisation benefit from some sort of training or programme on stress relief?

Some managers claim responsibility for avoiding burnout is borne by the individual worker. These managers are probably working in the organisations where burnout is a problem. As we have learned by now, workplace culture and communication play an enormous role in both burnout and productivity. It is the manager's role to increase productivity, which is best done via a communicative, effective, balanced work environment.

Anticipate the future and plan for it now

The most productive managers, both personally and for the organisation, learn to anticipate what will happen in the future and plan for it in advance. If you know your library will be filled with children for summer reading, you will schedule extra staff to deal with the larger crowds at the reference and circulation desks. If you learn that your state's budget is going downhill fast, you will begin to think about ways your library can cut money from its budget while preserving what is important as much as possible. Most of these things can be predicted by knowing and evaluating your library's services and role in the larger community. Managers are tasked with becoming aware of the very biggest picture of their organisation they can imagine. Keeping track of the history of the organisation and evaluating past and current services will help predict what will become successful or necessary in the future.

Planning for the future will prevent crisis management from taking hold. If you know in advance what to do in potential crises, such as with floods or pandemics, and communicate that knowledge well to your employees, they will be better prepared to deal with such instances. This is especially true for events that are not true crises. If you plan for and share information about upcoming events like summer reading or the start of the semester, then you and your employees will not have a chance to fall victim to crisis management cycles.

Luckily, librarianship has a great tradition of sharing information about services, assessment, budgeting and the like. This helps us plan better for the present as well as the future and gives us an excellent network of colleagues with whom we can discuss issues. Librarianship is one of the most forward-looking professions out there. Keep an ear out at conferences, keep up on professional reading and network with colleagues at other institutions, and envisioning the future can become much easier.

Much has been written and many classes and workshops are offered in management and organisation planning for the future. I recommend them to managers having trouble in this area. But as a basic rule: keep track of the past, plan strategically for your future, the profession's future and your organisation's future, and keep the lines of communication open and honest. In this way you can manage for productivity as well as preserve your own productivity. Productivity and good attitudes are contagious, especially when coming from above. The reverse is also true, but discord can start anywhere and harm an organisation quickly.

Questions to consider

- What is your preferred style and method of communication? What do your employees prefer?
- How do you prefer to be available to your employees?
- Are you a crisis manager? Is anyone in your library a crisis manager?

7

Sticking with productivity

With any change in how we do things, there is an adjustment period where we form new habits and get used to new ways of acting, planning and responding. It is normal to run into a few obstacles and need to rethink our productivity goals, plans and processes. These obstacles can be enough to derail a journey toward productivity. This chapter presents some tips and tricks for getting back on track.

Take your time

The best thing to remember is that becoming a more productive person takes time – quite a bit of time. Some guidelines suggest that it takes 30 days to set a habit and some suggest twice that amount. If you try to set a lot of new habits all at once, it will take longer and be more difficult. In general, you will want to aim for small, gradual changes over a set period of time, with firmly established and reasonable goals set concretely every few weeks. As we have learned so far, rushing is counter to productivity. If you want to do something well, it will need to be done slowly and thoughtfully, with an eye toward your overall goals.

When beginning, set a goal or two. Perhaps your goal is to check your e-mail only twice a day and spend only 30 minutes each time. Think about what tools you might need to meet this goal. For the e-mail goal, you will need a clock or timer. Set an end date for this goal to become a habit. The recommendation is to take at least a month. Once you have set this up, begin to incorporate your habit. Keep track of when you meet your goal each day. Keep track of why you did not meet your goal. At the end of the time period, review your log. How ingrained do you feel the habit has become? Have you found value in implementing the habit? Do you need another 30 days or some time period to focus on this one goal? Be gentle with yourself but also honest. Realise also that perhaps some habits or tips do not work out with your personality or current situation. If you feel frustrated after 30 days or do not see the value, consider dropping that goal and working on a different one.

It is usually best to work on only one or two habits at a time for a 30-day stretch. If you try to change your life or work style radically you may set yourself up for failure. And, just like with any goal, it helps to write down what change you are trying to make, and also your motivation for the change. You may want to write all this down then let it sit for a few days before beginning. This allows you to build a sort of anticipation around it that may motivate you.

You may also want to write down what obstacles you know you will face. Chances are you have tried to be more productive in the past without success. What caused problems then? Are there any situations that you encountered that send you into a flurry of procrastination, for example? It can help to make a plan ahead of time about how to deal with these obstacles before they arise.

Establishing a habit worksheet

Table 7.1 presents a worksheet template to help you establish your habit. Using this worksheet you can set forth

Table 7.1 A habit worksheet

Goal/habit to establish:	
Motivation/rationale for change:	
Expected obstacles and plan of attack:	
Timeline (weekly, daily, etc.):	Deadline:
Times I met this goal and what I gained:	Times I failed to meet the goal and why:

a plan closely tied to your overall goals and motivation, and track when you follow through and how that improves the situation, as well as when you fail and why.

Visualise the change

What do you expect the difference in your life will be when you adopt this habit? Having a vision of why you want to make a change can help you to be more successful. This may be another thing to write down, or, if you are artistic, you could draw it or make a collage or some other sort of representation. Making what you expect from the change more concrete makes it more real in some ways, and more achievable. Simply put, once you have pictured it, it feels more like it can happen. When I have felt overwhelmed and wanted to quit while writing this book, I have pictured myself giving my mom a copy of the finished product – the printed book. This was usually all I needed to stick with it for another day.

In line with visualisation of the positive outcome is the concept of positive self-talk. Be sure you are your number one booster when you are working on changing habits or completing a big project or meeting a goal. If you catch yourself thinking negative thoughts like, 'I will never get this chapter done!' be sure to replace that thought with your positive visualisation. It is cheesy, but if you are not on your own side rooting for victory, then nothing else matters.

Accountability is a virtue

A key method of sticking with a new habit or modifying behaviour in general is to make yourself accountable to another person. Recently there has been a rash of news stories about websites that will take your bet on whether you will meet certain goals, such as losing weight or quitting smoking. If you make your goal, some sites will pay out a modest fee. If you fail to meet your goal, however, you must pay a sum to the site. This type of incentive can be incredibly motivating. One of my colleagues has adopted her own version of this. Whenever she needs to accomplish something large, she designates a small sum of money and picks out a political cause she supports and one she hates. If she meets her goal, the money goes to the cause she supports. If she does not, she has to send money to support something she herself does not.

If you have a colleague or friend who also hopes to become more productive, you could team up to help each other stay on task and deal with obstacles. Chat every few days to see if there is some way you can aid each other with advice or encouragement. Compare accomplishments. Knowing that you will have to tell another person what you have been working on and how you are doing is a great motivator.

In the event that you do not work with or near someone who can share in this process, you can locate an online 'productivity buddy' from the library productivity community (*http://libraryproductivity.ning.com*). Members of this community can share their accomplishments and areas for improvement and receive or provide feedback as well.

Creating focus

The main goal of productivity systems and exercises is to get you into a place of focus, where you can create your best work without too much effort. This sense of focus, called 'the zone' by some, is the mental place where work flows without much effort. You feel confident in your situation and are unlikely to become distracted unless you are interrupted. Sometimes you can get lost in this productive state and glance at the clock only to surprise yourself at just how long you have been able to get things done.

Make sure again that your workplace is one that is conducive to working: uncluttered, with proper tools at hand and information filed away. Signs, pictures and the like can help you remember why you are doing what you do and keep your mind on track. One writer has suggested creating a mantra or slogan to remind yourself what you are trying to accomplish and why – maybe something like 'In by 8, out by 5' if you are trying to keep to a regular workday or get in earlier than usual.

Some people associate a certain mix of music with a task. I used to listen to a particular radio station when I did web design and just by turning it on I could get in the zone – my brain knew it was time to get to work. The power of a simple ritual like turning on certain music can awaken that focus.

Remember to take regular breaks to avoid burning out and to keep your focus fresh. Do not feel the need to force a break if you are in the zone, but make sure to tend to your basic needs, like food, stretching, and so on. It can also help to keep a fresh perspective by switching tasks after an hour or two. If you are able to keep in the zone, this can benefit some of your other work.

The media diet

Mentioned in Chapter 5 on systems, keeping a close eye on what kind of and how much media you consume can help with productivity, especially in terms of maintaining your focus. As far as your body is concerned, checking news and reading blogs and the like feels like work. It may seem to keep us informed but it can and often does become an unwise use of time and a tool for procrastination.

If you find yourself becoming more immersed in media at the expense of productive work, there are several steps you can try. The most extreme is to eliminate media consumption altogether for a period of time – a media fast. I did this on occasion when I needed more time and fewer distractions during the writing of this book. I found that I did not miss my morning reading of the *New York Times* and *Christian Science Monitor* as much as I thought I might and never did return to them. I also permanently stopped checking Google News throughout the day and listening to news in the car on the way to and from work. I still felt well informed and in fact felt a lot less stressed and more positive. I did return to watching television, but only for entertainment – no more news programmes other than long-form programmes like *Nova* and *Frontline*. I have begun to read a lot of books once more, but mostly for fun. I am still very tied to my Google

Reader, but have weeded out numerous current-event feeds that were redundant or no longer interesting.

Many people think that a media fast is the worst thing you can do. What will you miss? How will you ever catch up? The fact is, if something happens in the library world or the world at large that is important, you will hear about it via colleagues or family or friends. The only way to truly disconnect from media is to live like a hermit far away from people. I found that my colleagues and family served as trusted filters. If something was truly relevant and important, I heard about it even when I was on my media fast. For this reason, I have permanently reduced the amount of current events news I take in every day.

A less extreme version is to survey the media you use over the course of a week – internet sites, television watching, movies, magazines, books, social networks, games, music and everything else. We all know how much of a problem information overload is in the abstract, but when you start tallying it up, it may really surprise you. Try tracking your media diet for a week. Label your sources according to the recommended categories set up by Mark Hurst in *Bit Literacy*:

- *star sources*: these are the ones that give you just what you need and are the most helpful;

- *scan sources*: you usually find one or two useful nuggets of information but have to wade through some not-so-useful content to get there;

- *try out*: these are sources you are not yet sure about – you may be just adding them to the rotation to see what you get from them.

Any other type of source should be weeded out of your rotation. To evaluate, ask yourself what you gain from the source of information, whether you trust the source of information, and the ever-present question – whether it is worth your time.

The review process

Along the same lines as accountability, a strong review process can help keep you engaged and motivated. It creates accountability to yourself. This is a cornerstone of several of the systems discussed in the last chapter, for good reason. A review of activities, thoughts, incoming information and past and future goals helps ground our work in the big picture and shows that, even if we face some challenges, our momentum is carrying us forward step by step.

I recommend a review at the end of each day. Take a moment to jot down two or three accomplishments on your calendar or in a notebook kept for the purpose. Think about what you have to do tomorrow and make sure your calendar is up to date. Schedule necessary tasks to be completed and be sure you get a rest period or two. It can also help to outline the two or three major things that must be accomplished that next day. Sometimes getting out of the office can facilitate this process. Sit outside if the weather is nice enough, or maybe even just sit in a different part of the building. The change in physical perspective can sometimes help you see things differently. This process should take only about five to ten minutes, and the momentum you have provided for the next day is invaluable.

This review process should also be performed at the end of a week, fortnight or month as well, with a broader eye to goals and the bigger picture of your work. This review will take a half hour to an hour as you go over accomplishments from the time period, review your goals, think about new

Table 7.2	Template form to guide you through the review process

Review:
   Long-term/annual goals
   Shorter-term/weekly or monthly goals
   Incoming information and tasks
   Calendar for next week
   Running to-do lists
Next week's big goal(s):
   Monday
   Tuesday
   Wednesday
   Thursday
   Friday

directions and update to-do lists and calendars. An annual review, which is usually mandated by your place of work, is an excellent time for an even deeper evaluation. Take these opportunities seriously and you could find them a helpful tool in encouraging you to stick with productivity.

Both *Getting Things Done* and *Zen to Done* have excellent outlines for performing reviews. Both focus more on a weekly review where you take a look at long and short-term goals, look at incoming items, notes and tasks from the past week, look at your calendar for the next week and your to-do lists, and then set your goals and tasks for the coming week. Table 7.2 presents a template for a form to guide you through the process.

The mind dump

Related to the review but with a more unfortunate name, a mind dump can help you figure out what might be blocking you from being productive or sticking with a programme of productivity. The technique is very similar to that used to construct a to-do list in Chapter 3. Take out a pad of paper and a pen and write down everything that is on your mind – tasks, projects, goals, future dreams, personal and professional and anything in between. Sometimes this process can dislodge the thoughts or worries that have been blocking out productive activity. Once you have everything written down, process it all appropriately. Add 'to-do's to your list and update it. Update your goals. Rethink your day's structure. Check your calendar. Make sure the information you removed from your head is filed away properly or acted upon.

Flexibility

Recalling my diet example from the previous chapters, productivity, like dieting, is aided with a bit of flexibility. Sometimes you are stuck out on the road and have to eat whatever you can get, regardless of healthfulness. Sometimes a colleague calls in sick and your carefully planned day needs to be radically rethought. Developing a sense of flexibility regarding your time can help ease the stresses of a demanding workplace and help keep you productive even when your productive habits must be set aside to deal with minor emergencies.

This ties with giving up perfectionism, as discussed in Chapter 3 on procrastination. If you are able to accept that your schedule will never be perfect and you will never get every little thing done, this can help you relax and deal with what you can get done, rather than going completely off the rails any time an unexpected event comes along. In addition, you may need to become flexible with your definition of success as regards your goals. If your standards for success are too high, if you expect too much perfection from your goals, you will end up failing to achieve them.

As cheesy as it may sound, some simple stress-release exercises may come into good use here. My favourite is taking a deep breath. It can be done anytime and anywhere. When I am tempted to scrap my day's goals because I just got called to cover a reference desk shift, I take a deep breath and try to devote my whole attention to taking that breath. It takes less than 30 seconds to do, which is time anyone can spare. After that, I think about how I can still salvage my day. Can I take my work with me to the desk? Does it really need to be completed that day? Is there a colleague who can take on either the task or the desk shift? After taking a breath and a few seconds to think, I can usually see the opportunities where before I saw only more work.

Trust your system

As we discussed in the last chapter, a formal system may not be for everyone. But what does work for everyone is finding out what tips and tricks help you get things done and putting your trust in these tools. If making a to-do list at the end of the day is the perfect setup for the next day, be sure you follow through and put your faith in that habit. If you fail to perform a task like this for a few days, the trust you put in your system can sometimes pull you out of the inevitable desire to give up. Remind yourself that the tools did work and will work again if you renew your efforts.

Sticking with whatever system you derive for yourself will offer several of the same benefits as a more formal programme might. Simple is often better. Stick with what works for you for most of your situations. It helps to guide your actions in stressful or busy situations. It helps to answer the question, 'what do I do next?' It provides a basic structure to your time and reduces the universe of possible choices to a more manageable few.

Rewards revisited

As discussed in Chapter 2 on motivation, a reward can be a great incentive to stick with a new task, system or habit, and could help overcome feelings of stagnation or challenge. Rewarding yourself for following through on your commitment to productivity can emphasise that the habit itself is worthwhile and a positive experience. Even if the habit is an older one that has been forgotten for a time or has become onerous, a reward may be just the thing to refresh your mindset.

For a long-term goal or habit setting, use a schedule of rewards – a small reward for each of the first three days of implementing the habit, one at the end of each week, and then a big reward at the end of 30 days. To help create accountability and provide a tangible reminder of upcoming rewards, make a list for each habit/goal. For example:

- If I meet this goal for an entire day I will reward myself with this on the first three days...
- If I meet this goal for a whole week I will reward myself with this at the end of the week for the first three weeks...
- If I meet this goal for 30 days I will reward myself with this special reward...

Don't break the chain

Several productivity books and blogs relate the following story about Jerry Seinfeld, a notoriously hard worker. An up-and-coming comedian asked him about how he kept himself on task and working. He said he had a simple process. For every day that he wrote some material, he would put a large X on that date on his calendar. His goal was to keep the chain of Xs running as long as possible. He summed up the idea as, 'Don't break the chain'.

As shown with Seinfeld's string of Xs, we can use very simple measures to motivate us to stick with a new work habit or task. Consider, for example, the illustrative measures employed by fundraisers trying to reach a certain monetary point. You could use a similar bar graph or rising thermometer to reflect your contribution to a large project – the more you contribute, the higher up the bar goes. Such a measure could easily be adapted to a writing project like this book – the level increases as the word count goes up. It could also go up with number of reference questions answered, items catalogued, and so on. This can be a great visual motivational tool for a team working on a project that is in any way quantifiable. Witness the 'X days since an accident at this facility' signs you sometimes see, a similar idea that keeps people aware of the concept of workplace safety.

Resistance to change

When making changes, even positive ones, we all face some kind of trouble. It is important to remember that there will likely be ingrained and perhaps unconscious resistance to change. In *The War of Art*, Steven Pressfield characterises 'resistance' as the force that keeps us from performing our work and suggests that we 'go professional' to defeat it. What he means by this is that we take our creative work seriously and make a commitment to carrying it out. According to Pressfield, the first step to defeat resistance is to sit down to work. Doing this will likely make us miserable, but we still must do it.

Pressfield points out the subtle dangers of enthusiasm and love for your work, saying, 'The more you love your art/calling/ enterprise, the more important its accomplishment is to the evolution of your soul, the more you will fear it and the more resistance you will experience facing it' (Pressfield, 2002: 73). He calls on those who are facing resistance to:

- be patient;
- seek order;
- demystify work;
- act in the face of fear;
- accept no excuses;
- play it as it lays;
- be prepared;
- avoid showing off;
- keep a distance from mastery of technique;
- ask for help;
- employ the instrument but not become it;
- not to take failure or success personally;
- endure adversity;
- self-validate;
- recognise limitations;
- reinvent

The main concept is to create an image of yourself as worker, which you control and can change. Seeing yourself this way can be a powerful means to overcome the natural resistance to change in your work life and help you succeed in getting things done.

Should I quit?

Sometimes an inability to stick with something is a sign that you should not in fact stick with it, or that something else in your life needs to go to make room for the change. We discussed this a bit in Chapter 2 on motivation, but there is always room to quit a particular habit, task, behaviour or goal. As Seth Godin says in *The Dip*: 'Quit the wrong stuff. Stick with the right stuff. Have the guts to do one or the other' (Godin, 2007: 4). Godin goes on to explain that strategic quitting is essential to success.

The key to successful quitting, according to Godin, is to quit when things are stagnant. If you have to struggle a bit, you are in the eponymous dip right before you master a particular task or goal. Knowing that a struggle is actually a good thing, a learning experience, can help us re-evaluate what we might want to quit. Consider quitting a stagnant experience or one that does not offer growth in order to focus time and energy on the learning experience and the chance for eventual mastery. And if the learning experience and eventual mastery are not worth the time or effort, quit and find a learning experience that is.

Godin offers three questions to ask yourself when you are considering quitting:

- *Am I panicking?* In other words, is the decision to quit a well reasoned one or the easy way out?

- *Who am I trying to influence?* Are you dealing with just one person, who will just increase their resistance with each effort, or a larger group, which will tend to wear down with repeated tries?

- *What sort of measurable progress am I making?* You need to do more than survive your situation. If there is no forward progress, quitting may be a good idea.

The author further suggests, when taking on a new responsibility or adopting a new habit, writing down the conditions under which you would be ready to quit. This will prevent you from making a panicked decision.

Is that all there is?

As I said back in the first chapter, I am no paragon of productivity. I am good at getting things done, but I get just as overwhelmed, overworked, de-motivated, procrastination-prone, and just plain lazy as everyone else. Toward the end of this book I have felt pressured to increase production and have had to work some nights and weekends even though I laid out a good plan of action. I am in good company, however; even David Allen admits he is not a perfect adherent to *Getting Things Done*!

I have presented the tools I use and some that I have learned about along the way in the hope that they can help others as well. Productivity, like many things in life, is what you make of it, and the library community can surely benefit from working on these principles. I invite you to join the online community (*http://libraryproductivity.ning.com*), to join the discussion, learn from colleagues and share what wisdom you have as well.

Questions to consider

- What sort of problems have you had sticking with change in the past and how have you overcome them?
- What does your media diet look like? Is this an area you feel you might need to control better?
- What will you do next?

8

Resource guide

One thing I have learned over the course of this book is that productivity writers borrow heavily from one another. I have ensured that I have cited my sources when appropriate throughout the text, but what follows are the resources that I have found most valuable and/or interesting as I have worked on this book. Most of these resources repeat one another at some point, but I have tried to highlight what makes each unique.

General online resources

■ Community on Ning: *http://libraryproductivity.ning.com*

This website, created in support of the book you are currently reading, takes advantage of Web 2.0 technologies to allow us to share information about our own productivity situations. Find advice here and help out your colleagues. The site features a blog for productivity news of interest to library workers and forums for discussing everything related to becoming a better time manager.

■ Stepcase Lifehack: *http://www.lifehack.org*

Stepcase is a group blog devoted to 'lifehacks' – hints, tips and tricks to get things done by automating tasks, organising, and generally increasing productivity. Issues discussed include personal improvement, relationships, technology, and more.

■ Lifehacker: *http://lifehacker.com*

This is another group blog devoted to lifehacking. The originator of the blog, Gina Trapani, has authored a book on the subject based on the blog posts. The focus is on software and personal productivity but touches on personal improvement as well. There is a strong bend toward the practical as well, with posts that cover reducing utility bills and the best kitchen tools to buy.

■ FlyLady: *http://flylady.com*

This site is definitely targeted at homemakers and working women, with a strong focus on the home. However, there is plenty here on organisation of your workspace and inboxes to please the most devoted follower of *Getting Things Done*. Its personal approach and good advice for the slow integration of habits into your workflow may be just what you need to get organised.

■ 43 Folders: *http://www.43folders.com*

This is the website of Merlin Mann, a person who has made it his mission to help others find the time and attention to do their best creative work. This blog has a very personal feel and does an excellent job addressing creativity and productivity, something lacking in most other resources.

■ Put Things Off: *http://putthingsoff.com*

This website bills itself as 'laid-back advice for the idle generation'. It is a collection of articles by Nick Cernis, mostly about productivity, although a personal touch creeps in as well. He has also created some software applications for productivity and has written an e-book called Todoodlist (see under Procrastination).

Motivation

■ Shaw, C. (1992) 'A scientific solution to librarian burnout', *New Library World* 93(1103): 4–8.

This article proposes reducing symptoms of burnout among librarians through the adoption of transcendental mediation. It contains good basic information on identifying burnout and the benefit of applying transcendental meditation techniques, but not much on practical implementation of the techniques or on the techniques themselves.

Procrastination

■ Cernis, N. (n.d.) 'Toodoodlist: Technology is great. Pencils are greater', available at: *http://todoodlist.com/index.php* (accessed 26 January 2010).

The author has an amusing and interesting style in this e-book. The todoodlist is an interesting mind-map technique. The book expands the todoodlist into a loose system of productivity but the main emphasis is on to-do lists and paper technology.

■ Freeman, J. (2009) *The Tyranny of E-mail: The Four-Thousand-Year Journey to Your Inbox*, New York: Scribner.

This provides a fascinating history of mail and e-mail and a great discussion of the work and societal problems associated with the proliferation of e-mail.

Some to-do list tools to investigate

■ Remember the Milk (*http://www.rememberthemilk.com/*) – one of my favourites, also known as RTM. Integrates with Gmail and has an iPhone app. Very easy to use.

- HiTask (*http://hitask.com/*) – offers a simple free version with a fuller paid version that offers a lot of cross-functionality with software and devices like cell phones.

- TeuxDeux (*http://teuxdeux.com*) offers a weekly to-do list accessible on the web. Easy to use and usable.

- Deskaway (*http://www.deskaway.com/*) is built for teams and offers a 30-day trial of its service, which has a lot of great reporting features.

- Do.oh (*http://dopointoh.com/*) – simpler to use than RTM, but also very integrated with iPhone and web tools like Twitter and Facebook.

- Voo2do (*http://voo2do.com/*) – very similar to RTM but a bit more customisable.

- Basecamp (*http://basecamp.com*) – a full-blown project management solution with a price tag to match. Very well regarded, however.

- Backpack (*http://backpackit.com*) – also a business-solution oriented tool for project management and sharing. Not free.

- Ta-da List (*http://tadalist.com*) –free, simple and sharable. A very simple version of Backpack from the same people.

- Nozbe (*http://nozbe.com*) – a browser-based project management tool for individuals and businesses. Not free but very affordable. Has a lot of flexibility with applications, plans and prices.

- Get Back To Work (*http://www.marktaw.com/getbacktowork .htm*) – through this site you can enter a task and a deadline and keep the window open in the background. As you meet or miss deadlines, you return to the window and check the appropriate box, then enter new tasks. You can keep track of your whole day easily with a handy tally of how many goals you meet or miss.

Time management

- Jacobs, A. J. (2009) 'How I stopped the multitasking madness: one man's quest to go from manic multitasker to zen unitasker in one month flat', *Real Simple* 10(9): 198–202.

A humour writer takes on his multitasking habit. One of my favourite tricks that he tried was narrating his actions out loud. This is definitely an effective way to maintain focus on what you are doing.

- Sheridan, L. (2009) 'Harnessing time: Empowering staff in the workplace', *Library Management* 30(6/7): 369–82.

The managers at this particular library instituted a professional development time where employees, after an application process, were given 3.5 hours of uninterrupted time to work on a particular project. Workers found it hard to work without distractions and also discovered that even 3.5 hours were not enough to get needed tasks done. I was amazed that they had to apply to get 3.5 uninterrupted hours!

- Pausch, R. (2007) 'Time management', speech presented at University of Virginia, Charlottesville, 28 November, available at: *http://video.google.com/videoplay?docid=-5784740380335567758* (accessed 26 January 2010).

Dr Pausch, author of *The Last Lecture*, was diagnosed with pancreatic cancer in 2006. His fight against the disease and his use of his remaining time was nothing short of inspirational. In this lecture, Dr Pausch shared his personal tips for time management, something that became acutely important for him after his diagnosis. Dr Pausch passed away on 25 July 2008.

Calendaring tools

- Google Calendar (*http://calendar.google.com*) – my personal favourite. Very easy to use and integrates with all Google services.

- Yahoo Calendar (*http://calendar.yahoo.com*) – a good choice if you use a Yahoo e-mail address.

- 30 Boxes (*http://30boxes.com/*) – well-designed and nice to look at. Very sharable.

- Plaxo (*http://www.plaxo.com*) – excellent for sharing. I used Plaxo for a while in an elaborate hack to get my Outlook and Google calendars to synch.

Reminder tools

- PingMe (*http://gopingme.com*) – send alerts to your e-mail or phone to remind you of tasks or appointments. Can go off repeatedly until you tell them to stop.

Time tracking sites

- Toggl (*http://toggl.com*) – a simple online time tracker, often used by those who bill hours, but also good for tracking what you do throughout the day.

- Rescue Time (*http://www.rescuetime.com/*) – does a similar thing but is software-based and monitors what applications you actually use on your computer.

Systems

The main works on productivity systems that I examined in depth are:

- Allen, D. (2001) *Getting Things Done: The Art of Stress-Free Productivity*, New York: Penguin Books.

- Babauta, L. (2008) 'Zen to done: The ultimate productivity system', available at: *http://zenhabits.net/2007/11/zen-to-done-the-simple-productivity-e-book/* (accessed 26 January 2010).

- Covey, S. (1989) *The Seven Habits of Highly Successful People: Restoring the Character Ethic*, New York: Simon and Schuster.

- Ferriss, T. (2007) *The 4-Hour Workweek: Escape 9–5, Live Anywhere, and Join the New Rich*, New York: Crown Publishers.

- Hurst, M. (2007) *Bit Literacy: Productivity in the Age of Information and E-mail Overload*, New York: Good Experience Press.

- Leeds, R. (2009) *One Year to an Organized Work Life: From Your Desk to Your Deadlines, the Week-by-Week Guide to Eliminating Office Stress for Good*, Philadelphia, PA: Da Capo Press.

- Morgenstern, J. (2004) *Never Check Email in the Morning and other Unexpected Strategies for Making Your Work Life Work*, New York: Simon and Schuster.

Others that might be of interest:

- Allen, D. (2003) *Ready for Anything: 52 Productivity Principles for Work and Life*, New York: Penguin.

Fresh off the bestselling rise of *Getting Things Done*, David Allen wrote another, lesser known, bestseller on many of the same topics. This book contains short essays and has more of a personal approach. Chapters also feature checklists for thinking about concepts and completing activities.

- Allen, D. (2008) *Making it all Work: Winning at the Game of Work and the Business of Life*, New York: Viking.

This book was billed as the next lesson for *Getting Things Done*. It expands on the lessons and techniques taught in that book, with a special focus on perspective and planning.

- Babauta, L. (2009) *The Power of Less: The Fine Art of Limiting Yourself to The Essential...in Business and in Life*, New York: Hyperion.

Also capturing the popularity of his system and blog, Leo Babauta has written a traditional print book on simplifying your life. While it is less of a rehash than Allen's book, it still contains many of the same core concepts but with a fuller focus on simplicity.

- Brooks, W. (1989) *High Impact Time Management*, Englewood Cliffs, NJ: Prentice-Hall.

This book presents a different approach to time management, based on understanding the value of time, understanding the tools of time management, and practice in using the tools of time management. It contains a 'unique and copyrighted Time Analysis Grid' and references the rising productivity of Japan in an effort to motivate readers. It contains a great chapter on crisis management and how to avoid it.

- Cirillo, F. (2007) 'The Pomodoro Technique', available at: *http://www.pomodorotechnique.com/resources/cirillo/The PomodoroTechnique_v1-3.pdf* (accessed 26 January 2010).

This work is mentioned in Chapter 3 on procrastination and I thought about covering it as a system as well. I decided against this, however, as it is far simpler than any of the systems I did examine, although that could be a definite strength. The book also includes some forms for organising your to-do list and recording your victories.

- Clark, J. and Clark, S. (1992) *Prioritize, Organize: The Art of Getting it Done*, Shawnee Mission, KS: National Press Publications.

Meant to serve as a 'user manual', this book has great tips for getting motivated and getting things done.

- Cooper, J. (1971) *How to Get More Done in Less Time*, New York: Doubleday.

This book could have been titled, 'How We Got This Way'. It has a heavy focus on the benefits of multitasking and is fairly sexist to boot. The author talks extensively about the monetary value of time, considered from the organisation's perspective. I recommend it just to demonstrate how far we have come and how much has changed in the workplace and society at large.

- Crenshaw, D. (2008) *The Myth of Multitasking: How 'Doing it All' Gets Nothing Done*, San Francisco, CA: Jossey-Bass.

This book is really a short parable on the failings of multitasking, which it calls 'switch-tasking', as you must switch your attention frequently. An interesting thing about this work is that it says meetings can boost productivity, as they prevent time being stolen via interruptions. This is a different stance from almost every other guide I read, which nearly universally deride meetings as a waste of time.

- Douglass, M. and Douglass, D. (1980) *Manage Your Time, Manage Your Work, Manage Yourself*, New York: American Management Associations.

According to this book, time management is really self-management. It begins with a very interesting analysis of time from a cultural and personal perspective. Unfortunately a bit dated, it assumes secretarial support for most functions and almost all examples are males.

- Kendrick, J. and Kendrick, J. (1988) *Personal Productivity: How to Increase your Satisfaction in Living*, Armonk, NY: M. E. Sharpe.

Despite being published at the end of the 1980s, this book is still very sexist. It assumes the reader is male and has a wife to take care of domestic duties. It has a big focus on financial management, a change from many other books I read.

- Kirn, W. (2007) 'The autumn of the multitaskers', *The Atlantic* 300(4): 66–80, available at: *http://www.theatlantic .com/doc/print/200711/multitasking* (accessed 26 January 2010).

This is a rather well-known article about the risks of multitasking, told from a personal perspective. The article focuses particularly on gadgets.

- Molloy, J. (1987) *How to Work the Competition into the Ground and Have Fun Doing It: A Proven Program to Raise your Personal Productivity*, New York: Warner Books.

This book is not especially well written but distinguishes itself by openly using the same techniques that cults use to brainwash followers to help you persuade yourself to adopt productivity skills.

- Pollar, O. (1992) *Organizing Your Workspace: A Guide to Personal Productivity*, Los Altos, CA: Crisp Publications.

This book has a strong focus on the physical workspace and eliminating clutter. It assumes a paper-based work environment and is thus a bit old-fashioned; however it does have very good advice on decluttering.

- *Results-Driven Manager: Taking Control of Your Time* (2005) Boston, MA: Harvard Business School Publishing Corporation.

This book has 16 chapters, mostly written by different authors. The chapters on 'infoglut' and burnout are especially well written but others are fairly standard.

- Winston, S. (2004) *Organized for Success: Top Executives and CEOs Reveal the Organizing Principles that Helped them Reach the Top*, New York: Crown Business.

An analysis of successful CEOs, as the name implies, this book hits the major issues. There are no major unifying themes but it is a good read and provides insight into how productive people operate.

Articles on the application of *Seven Habits*

As promised in Chapter 5, here are some articles that discuss *Seven Habits*.

- 'Confessor to the boardroom' (1996) *Economist* 338(7954): 74.

While not the most scholarly of works, this article analyses Stephen Covey's credentials and qualifications. It tackles his effect on the business world and also his own business acumen.

- Heitschmidt, R. (1996) 'Credibility and the business of range professionals', *Rangelands* 18(6): 234–7.

The author of this article applies *Seven Habits* to range professionals (those who manage public and private lands for livestock). The article is a very interesting application of the principles to a profession.

- Jones, C. (2005) 'Wisdom paradigms for the enhancement of ethical and profitable business practices', *Journal of Business Ethics* 57: 363–75.

This article says that businesses should not waste time trying to invent new models, but instead focus on other paradigms based on 'wisdom.' Covey's works provide the framework for the theory of wisdom that is examined.

- Perlow, L. (1999) 'The time famine: Toward a sociology of work time', *Administrative Science Quarterly* 44: 57–81.

The *Seven Habits* books are discussed in an analysis of framing individuals' work patterns in larger societal contexts.

General articles and books of interest

- Bell, S. (2009) 'What academic libraries contribute to productivity', *Library Journal*, 13 August, available at: *http://www.libraryjournal.com/article/CA6676486.html* (accessed 26 January 2010).

The author discusses academic productivity as a financial measure: state spending per degree conferred. He proposes that academic libraries contribute a great deal to the productivity of the institution via services delivered, and emphasises that we will need to demonstrate our quantifiable worth in this atmosphere.

- Carnegie, D. (1998) *Dale Carnegie's Lifetime Plan for Success: How to Win Friends and Influence People, How to Stop Worrying and Start Living*, New York: Galahad Books.

This handy volume combines two of Carnegie's bestsellers and is essential for ideas on how best to communicate in the business world.

- Griessman, B. E. (1994) *Time Tactics of Very Successful People*, New York: McGraw-Hill.

A fairly standard guide to time management, this book is a compilation of hints and anecdotes organised by topic. It has great advice on finding hidden time and how to know when to quit tasks.

- Jones, J. (1992) *High-Speed Management: Time-Based Strategies for Managers and Organizations*, San Francisco, CA: Jossey-Bass.

This book is rather dated – it keeps referring to the upcoming future of the late 1990s – but contains valuable advice on how to make your workplace more productive from a managerial perspective.

- Seiss, J. (2002) *Time Management, Planning and Prioritization for Librarians*, Lanham, MD: Scarecrow Press.

I discovered this book six weeks before my book's deadline and thought, 'Oh, no, it's all been done!' However, this book focuses specifically on special libraries and one-person libraries and is written in a very different style. It features excellent tips and tricks, especially on planning and prioritisation.

- Townsend, B. and Rosser, V. (2007) 'Workload issues and measures of faculty productivity', *Thought and Action: The NEA Higher Education Journal* 23: 7–20.

A discussion of productivity as it applies to teaching faculty. Workload issues are confined to teaching workload and productivity is measured for the most part in scholarly output. Interestingly, some states track faculty productivity as a measurement of the efficacy of an institution. All types of higher education institutions demonstrated higher workloads and more productivity when comparing 2004 levels with 1993 levels.

- Tracy, B. (2004) *Time Power: A Proven System for Getting More Done in Less Time than You Ever Thought Possible*, New York: American Management Association.

This book is written in a bombastic style, meant to energise the reader into taking action. Each chapter includes action exercises to implement time management strategies right away. The book offers much guidance for business managers but does not offer much that is new.

- Trapani, G. (2008) *Upgrade Your Life: The Lifehacker Guide to Working Smarter, Faster, Better*, Indianapolis, IN: Wiley.

This book, written by the creator of the popular Lifehacker blog, organises and dispenses some of the most popular blog posts in a non-electronic format. Well-organised into topics, each of the 116 'hacks' offers a solution to a common productivity problem, from dealing with e-mail to managing multiple computers to organising files. There is a heavy emphasis on technology and its use.

The final word

- *Onion* (2007) 'Study finds working at work improves productivity', available at: *http://www.theonion.com/content/node/69238* (accessed 26 January 2010).

As usual, *The Onion* cuts right to the chase – the best way to be productive is to actually work at work. This article is highly recommended.

9

Wrapping up

As I type this, it is early January. I managed to finish the bulk of this book before Christmas and took a genuine two-week long holiday at the end of the year. This was the longest vacation, other than a short stint of unemployment, that I have ever taken since graduating from high school over ten years ago. What made it a true holiday was the fact that I spent most of it at home, doing nothing but enjoying time with my family.

Then reality intruded – it was time to return to work. However, when I finally returned to my office, I found it hard to truly return to work. The past year had been filled with many projects with firm deadlines, and big goals I had set for myself had come to fruition. Now I was facing a new year with no looming tasks and no set goals. Nothing had to be done immediately, and an impending reorganisation at my place of work discouraged me from taking on any new projects right away. I found myself drifting and at loose ends.

I realised that this was an ideal situation to test out what I set forth in this very book. I was lacking motivation, to say the least, and recognised I could use some improvement of my time management and task organisation. I definitely needed a refresher on sticking with productivity.

My first step was to set some new goals. I reread my chapter on motivation and thought a bit about what I wanted to accomplish with my career. I looked at some job listings to get a feel for what other libraries were doing with their open positions. I gleaned some ideas from these about what sort of things my workplace could do and what I could do with my career if I were to leave my place of work. Even if you are not actively looking for another job, keeping tabs on the current marketplace helps you keep perspective on your own position, encourages you to keep yourself current in your field, and establishes a base of knowledge about what other institutions are doing. This can be invaluable should you lose your job, have to move, or just want a new challenge.

I went through a personal SWOT exercise, where I wrote down my strengths, weaknesses, opportunities and threats. It was a good opportunity to get reacquainted with myself and my current position, especially given the upcoming reorganisation. A SWOT exercise is great for refocusing and thinking differently about your skills and your position in your workplace. To do one, divide a piece of paper into quadrants and label each of the four: strengths, weaknesses, opportunities and threats. Write down your personal and career strengths and weaknesses in the appropriate quadrants, and the threats and opportunities from your current position in those quadrants. This exercise is only valuable if you are honest and open about your strengths and weaknesses, of course.

I found that I still love to do what I was hired to do and that I am working in a position which takes advantage of my strengths. I realised late last year that I am stretched too thin, however, in my current position. I have too many responsibilities given the time I have available. This is something that I hope will be corrected in the upcoming reorganisation. Reducing or redistributing some of my responsibilities would go a long way toward reducing my risk for burnout, I noted, and I shared this information with the library director and director of human resources. I also learned that there are employment opportunities out there for me, even in this down economy, which helped me feel more valuable.

Feeling slightly more solid in my profession and position, I felt more motivated to do good work while on the clock rather than restlessly drift through the day. My work feels more fulfilling now and I see more possibilities for defining and proposing meaningful tasks and projects. This should help me provide more value to the upcoming reorganisation process and in turn make me more useful in the process.

In the meantime, however, I did have a few tasks to get done during the month, including finishing this final chapter. I decided with the New Year to revamp my time management and task management processes. As a die-hard technology geek, I went with paper tools to shake up my thinking about productivity and time management. As I described earlier, doing familiar tasks a different way can help get you out of a productivity slump.

As a fan of David Seah's Printable CEO series (*www.davidseah.com/pceo/*), I adopted a new day-planner structure from his website, which he calls the Emergent Task Planner. I have never before taken an entire sheet of paper to plan my day, but I find that with all that space to fill I am more enthused to complete it with needed tasks and the occasional dreaded meeting. It gives me enough space to stretch out and be very specific about what I hope to accomplish during the day.

Paired with this, I have started to use David Seah's Task Project Tracker document, as a new to-do list manager. I have defined loose project areas such as 'instruction', 'writing' and 'service', and list out my tasks for each area. Again, the paper list gives me a bit more freedom than I felt I previously had with my online tool. With paper it is easy to jot down notes when the mood strikes me, without firing up a program or logging into a website. Tracking tasks in a new way helps my brain think differently about connections and approaches to tasks that may have gone a bit stale after five years in the same position.

Using paper after so many years online and plugged in has been a challenge. I have forgotten my notebook for nearly every meeting so far, but when I do bring it I enjoy the ease of seeing what else I have scheduled for the coming weeks, bundled with my to-do list/task tracker, my goal-planning and setting documents, and a calendar for the entire year printed out on one sheet. This calendar has been a special help for planning long-term projects, to see the entire year at a glance.

It is too soon to say if I will give up some of my online tools permanently in favour of paper. For one thing, my place of work still requires me to keep an Outlook calendar on my computer. For another, I have grown accustomed to looking at my calendar and to-dos from any computer, rather than having to remember to carry a notebook. If nothing else, getting me to think about how I spend my day in a new light will be worthwhile even if the new way of tracking my time does not persist.

Speaking of tracking my time, I have also begun a time audit as I recommended in Chapter 3 on procrastination. I had a feeling I was taking more time than was necessary. I learned that e-mail, once checked no more than twice a day for a half-hour period, has crept back into my daily activities far more than I recommend. Some days I was spending nearly three hours, here and there, working on e-mail. It is very easy to fritter away the better part of a day sending, receiving, reading and filing e-mail as it feels so much like work.

I also found myself giving up my proscribed lunchtime to deal with e-mail – a double-whammy to productivity. I should know better than to give up my break time for a needless task like e-mail. I have forced myself to crack down on both yet again. E-mail will always be a challenge to all of us, but it can be so easy to control once a good procedure is in place.

This review served as an excellent reminder to trust in the time-management system that I set up for myself. As I described in Chapter 7 on sticking with productivity, it can be very easy to fall off the path of productivity. When you get out of certain habits, for example during my vacation, it can be hard to pick them back up. You may feel a bit of despair and panic as you attempt to get back on schedule. But once I started back up with my calendar and task management, I felt much more in control of my time. Following my trusted system, even after a break from it, will restore sanity to my work life, even if it seems an impossible task at the start.

I also found inspiration in a new book, *Drive: The Surprising Truth about what Motivates Us* by Daniel H. Pink (2009). This book presents a concept the author calls Motivation 3.0. Rather than focus on rewards and punishments, the author claims we need to 'upgrade to autonomy, mastery and purpose'. People desire to direct their own work and lives, and need to have a purpose that serves something larger than them, in order to improve and be productive. For creative work, like the work that many library workers perform, a 'carrot and stick' reward structure does not foster excellent work. Creative work responds much better if those performing it have the autonomy to choose how, when, where and with whom it is done. Those performing work need to know why the work is important and how it serves a larger purpose.

In our upcoming reorganisation, I am attempting to promote the restructure of our workplace along these lines. I have recommended the book vociferously to everyone involved in the process. If you are in the lucky position of affecting how your workplace is managed and employees are motivated, this book provides excellent insight into new ways to produce creative work at a high level all around. However, as the restructuring drags on, I am not certain how much of this change will actually be a change rather than a reshuffling. We can only affect our own spheres of influence, and sometimes my sphere seems to be a bit smaller than I would like.

In the end, the only way to commit personally to productivity was to just do some work. I avoided writing this very chapter for over a week. Putting my thoughts down on paper seemed insurmountable. I had so many other things to do. I had so many other things I wanted to do! But once I finally made myself sit down and write for an hour, I wrote most of this chapter in just one sitting. Getting started can be the hardest part, so I hope this book has given you some tips to help you do just that and discover your more productive self.

Bibliography

Scientific American Mind (2006) 'The burnout cycle', *Scientific American Mind* 17(3), available at: *http://search .ebscohost.com* (accessed 24 August 2009).

Abaté, C. (2008) 'You say multitasking like it's a good thing', *Thought & Action: The NEA Higher Education Journal* 24: 7–13.

Allen, D. (2001) *Getting Things Done: The Art of Stress-Free Productivity*, New York: Penguin Books.

American Library Association (2009) 'ALA Library Fact Sheet Number 6', available at: *http://ala.org/ala/aboutala/ offices/library/libraryfactsheet/alalibraryfactsheet6.cfm* (accessed 27 August 2009).

Babauta, L. (2008) 'Zen to done: The ultimate productivity system', available at: *http://zenhabits.net/2007/11/zen-to-done-the-simple-productivity-e-book/* (accessed 26 January 2010).

Bell, S. (2005) 'The Infodiet: How libraries can offer an appetizing alternative to Google', *Chronicle of Higher Education* 50(24): B15.

Carnegie, D. (1998) *Dale Carnegie's Lifetime Plan for Success: How to Win Friends & Influence People, and How to Stop Worrying and Start Living*, New York: Galahad Books.

Covey, S. (1989) *The Seven Habits of Highly Successful People: Restoring the Character Ethic*, New York: Simon & Schuster.

Crenshaw, D. (2008) *The Myth of Multitasking: How 'Doing It All' Gets Nothing Done*, San Francisco, CA: Jossey-Bass.

Ferriss, T. (2007) *The 4-hour Workweek: Escape 9–5, Live Anywhere, and Join the New Rich*, New York: Crown Publishers.

Freeman, J. (2009) *The Tyranny of E-mail: The Four Thousand Year Journey to Your Inbox*, New York: Simon & Schuster.

Godin, S. (2007) *The Dip: A Little Book that Teaches you When to Quit (and When to Stick)*, New York: Penguin.

Hofstadter, D. (1999) *Gödel, Escher, Bach: An Eternal Golden Braid*, New York: Basic Books.

Hurst, M. (2007) *Bit Literacy: Productivity in the Age of Information and E-mail Overload*, New York: Good Experience Press.

Jacobs, A. J. (2009) 'How I stopped the multitasking madness: one man's quest to go from manic multitasker to zen unitasker in one month flat', *Real Simple* 10(9): 198–202.

Kotler, S. (2009) 'Escape artists', *Psychology Today* 42(5): 72–9.

Leeds, R. (2009) *One Year to an Organized Work Life: From your Desk to your Deadlines, the Week-by-Week Guide to Eliminating Office Stress for Good*, Philadelphia, PA: Da Capo Press.

Morgenstern, J. (2004) *Never Check Email in the Morning and other Unexpected Strategies for Making your Work Life Work*, New york: Simon & Schuster.

Pink, D. H. (2009) *Drive: The Surprising Truth about what Motivates You*, New York: Riverhead Books.

Pressfield, S. (2002) *The War of Art: Break Through the Blocks and Win Your Inner Creative Battles*, New York: Warner Books.

Schraw, G., Wadkins, T. and Olafson, L. (2007) 'Doing the things we do: A grounded theory of academic procrastination', *Journal of Educational Psychology* 99(1): 12–25.

Index

routine, 23–4, 58–61, 71, 94
ritual, 121

Seah, David 149
Seinfeld, Jerry, 128–9
SMART goals, 13
stress, 21–4, 38, 126–7
success, xvii, 106–7, 115–16, 119,
    126, 130–1
supervisors, 9, 15, 18, 28, 33,
    48–9, 51, 66–7, 72, 103–16
support system, 20, 37, 82
SWOT analysis, 148

tasks, breaking down, 13, 19–20,
    47–9
tickler file, 86
TRAF, 30, 43
trust, 104–7, 127–8, 151

value of time, 63, 88, 140–1
visualisation, 20, 39, 83, 119–20,
    128–30

willpower, 41, 44
workflow, 58–61
workspaces, 29–31

Breinigsville, PA USA
23 March 2011
258301BV00003B/2/P